THE
NAUTICAL
PREPPER

THE NAUTICAL PREPPER

How to Equip and Survive on Your Bug-Out Boat

Capt. William E. Simpson II

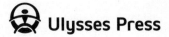 Ulysses Press

Published in the U.S. by
ULYSSES PRESS
P.O. Box 3440
Berkeley, CA 94703
www.ulyssespress.com

ISBN: 978-1-61243-220-5
Library of Congress Control Number 2013938284

Printed in the United States by United Graphics Inc.

10 9 8 7 6 5 4 3 2 1

Contributing Writer: Michael Kasten
Acquisitions Editor: Kelly Reed
Managing Editor: Claire Chun
Editors: Bill Cassel, Leslie Tilley
Proofreader: Elyce Berrigan-Dunlop
Cover design: what!design @ whatweb.com
Cover graphics: sailing on water © Barnaby Chambers/shutterstock
    .com; city © f9photos/shutterstock.com
Interior illustrations: © Kasten Marine Design, Inc.
Layout and production: Lindsay Tamura

Distributed by Publishers Group West

Contents

Preface

The world today is a vastly different place than it was in years past. Economic, social, and political situations worldwide have created an uncertain future for modern civilization and society as we know it. Added to those uncertainties are others that are well beyond our control: the forces of nature.

Recently, we have witnessed the events following regional-scale natural disasters such as hurricanes Sandy and Katrina, which left millions of people without electrical power. Shortages of food and fresh water quickly precipitated civil unrest and competition for resources. These and other events bear witness to the validity of the concerns that many people feel today.

As if that wasn't enough to be concerned about, according to leading scientists and engineers, the potential for a widespread collapse of the North American electrical grid poses the largest single risk to civilization as we know it today. According to several recent government and civilian reports[1], the most credible imminent threat

---

1   Report of the Commission to Assess the Threat to the United States from Electromagnetic Pulse (EMP) Attack

to modern civilization is the collapse of the electrical grid caused by damage from a geomagnetic storm or by a high-altitude electromagnetic pulse (HEMP) attack perpetrated by terrorists or a rogue nation.

Of course, other scenarios could also lead to wide-spread chaos and social disruption on an unprecedented scale.

In response to these uncertainties and in light of the potential for violent competition by unprepared survivors for basic resources, millions of people[2] are stockpiling supplies and guns in shelters and underground bunkers, many of which are remotely located. Some families have even gone so far as to engage in paramilitary style training. This training—where even children have been equipped with firearms such as assault rifles—is in anticipation of the armed combat that may be required for families to protect themselves from hoards of violent survivors. Reality TV shows call these people "preppers," and several of these TV shows, including National Geographic's *Doomsday Preppers,* feature weekly prime-time episodes depicting preppers and their preparations for various disasters.

On the other hand, the Federal Emergency Management Agency (FEMA) has its own recommendations, which include three days' worth of food and water, along with other items such as flashlights, whistles, moist towelettes, garbage bags, and a first aid kit, but no weapons.

---

2 http://www.dailymail.co.uk/news/article-2099714/Meet-preppers-Up-3-MILLION-people-preparing-end-world-know-it.html?ito=feeds-newsxml

In light of recent disasters where millions of people went without food, water, and power, in many cases for weeks, FEMA's advice seems inadequate to address people's actual needs during such events.

This begs the question: Why not simply adopt a more reasonable and effective approach that doesn't require paramilitary tactics or weapons and provides long-term sustainability for families during such events?

I believe it's a mistake to devise a general survival solution based upon a single potential disaster event. Instead, why not devise a survival plan that addresses as many possible scenarios as is practical. Based on my actual experience of living comfortably off the grid long term at remote, uninhabited desert islands, this book is intended to provide readers with critical strategic and tactical information, including key survival tools that can help anyone improve their survival planning and preparedness.

Some people think of hardships when the word *survival* is used. My objective with this book to offer a unique approach to being prepared and surviving that will minimize, and in many cases eliminates, the hardships that some other methods seem to embrace. And through this alternative survival paradigm the need for planned armed combat is negated.

My experience in expedition sailing and living off the grid comes from more than two decades of operating as a professional mariner, as well as two multiyear sailing expeditions with my family and friends. As a result, many of the methods and solutions that I am proffering have successfully evolved from operational group dynamics. During the course of those long-range expeditions—one from 1991 to 1994 and the other from 2010 to 2011—my wife and I, our children, and our dogs sailed to remote island locations and lived comfortably, totally off the grid. We tested all kinds of equipment and methods for survival; used solar and wind power to augment our power needs; and significantly augmented our food stores by fishing and collecting lobsters, mollusks, and seaweed from the waters around our tropical island retreats. I firmly believe that with proper guidance and a good boat, most people could enjoy the same success during an actual crisis—or just to experience an amazing adventure.

CHAPTER 1
Prepare Your Mind

Imagine waking up one morning to discover that you overslept because your alarm clock didn't go off. And as you examine the clock you realize it's not working, but why? You climb out of bed and go to the light switch on the wall and flip it on. No light. Thinking it must be a circuit breaker, you head to the panel and find all the breakers are in the "on" position. It's then you notice that some of your neighbors are wandering around outside, some huddled together in anxious conversation—about what, you wonder?

Walking into the living room, you switch on the TV out of habit, forgetting that the power is off. Then you grab your smartphone, only to find it's also malfunctioning. Finally you dig out the old battery-powered radio that's in the hall closet and flip it on—but it also fails to work.

Now you start to worry—*What the hell?* Finally you throw on some clothes and go outside and join your neighbors, who are all just as mystified as you are. As more people join it, nobody has any answers and the fear starts to become palpable. You hear one neighbor yelling to another: *My car won't start, how about yours? Nothing works! Shit!* A young couple who rode their bicycles into town earlier have just returned and are visibly frightened. You join some of the others rushing over to them and ask *What's happened? What's going on?* They respond that the whole town is down, and everyone is on foot or riding bikes, no cars are moving anywhere. Nobody knows what's happened or what to do. Even the police are walking around looking lost. They're telling people to stay calm but everyone is spooked. The couple says, *We could hear glass breaking at some storefronts down the street … We're scared!*

At this point in our imaginary scenario, it may be less than 24 hours until most people realize they are on their own and armed conflict over resources begins. That's not much time to react, and this is where being mentally prepared pays off. The people who have a plan in place and quickly make the right decisions in these critical early hours after a catastrophic event will greatly increase their chances for survival.

This kind of scenario could overtake any of our lives with little or no warning. And if you are not prepared, then you end up desperate, like the thousands of unprepared people who became the victims of hurricanes Katrina and Sandy.

The key to survival after any disaster—fire, storm, nuclear, EMP—is being prepared, and that means being prepared at all levels, including mentally.

Some people dismiss the potential risks, saying, *Oh, that will never happen here,* or, *That will never happen in our lifetime,* or *That can't happen here because our government will protect us.* These same people will be impacted the most by almost any disaster. And sadly, many of these same people, being the least prepared, will likely become part of the problems that will ensue, as they have in almost every historical case. Like a drowning man who cannot swim and grabs onto those who can, pulling them under, these people pose a genuine risk to those people who have gone to the time, trouble, and expense to be ready for the worst.

Being prepared to deal with thousands upon thousands of displaced disaster victims—what preppers call "unprepared people or zombies"—is supposed to be the job of the government, not individual citizens. But in the case of a high-altitude electromagnetic pulse (HEMP) attack or severe geomagnetic storm, the government, according to its own studies and reports[3], will also immediately be reduced to a pre-industrial status. In other words, nearly everyone will be on their own. Look at 2012's Hurricane Sandy and the ensuing events in New York and New Jersey: millions of people without electricity, fuel, food, or water, and many without any real shelter for several weeks. Major portions of New York City were dark at night for over a week, and in the blackness of the night, looting, assaults, and rapes were prevalent[4]. And this was merely a localized event that did not affect most of the major

---

3 Report of the Commission to Assess the Threat to the United States from Electromagnetic Pulse (EMP) Attack

4 www.safehorizon.org/index/get-involved-14/events-107/hurricane-sandy-your-support-at-work-355.html
www.alaskadispatch.com/article/after-hurricane-sandy-looting-fights-and-other-crimes
http://www.examiner.com/article/sandy-looting-arrests-after-hurricane-nyc

nearby cities, yet help was not immediately forthcoming, and when help did arrive it was largely ineffective. There was one report that alleged FEMA didn't even arrive until four days after Sandy hit, and ran out of drinking water on the same day! They also had great difficulty providing adequate quantities of generators that worked[5]. Imagine if the disaster were more widespread and this scenario extended across the United States and Canada—who's coming to help then? *Nobody* is the likely answer.

Practice Makes Permanent

We practice things like fire drills on land and on board ships for a reason. When unexpected things happen, to survive you must react quickly and correctly to the situation, without having to think about it. You simply don't have time to have a committee meeting to figure out what to do.

Preparedness training drills teach you to react correctly to a given situation, and by practicing and reviewing them often, your reactions can become second nature. This alone is a big advantage in any disaster. Knowing what to do allows you to make the best use of the critically compressed timeline that most disaster scenarios entail.

The first step to being truly prepared is preparing your mind. You can begin that process by spending some time studying various past disasters, including things like the Carrington Event of 1859, named for the British scientist

---

5   http://washingtonexaminer.com/fema-and-disaster-socialism/
    article/2513009
    http://online.wsj.com/article/SB1000142405297020470710457809 3
    192471666514.html

Richard Carrington, who observed and documented that massive solar storm. This was a severe geomagnetic storm that caused telegraph wires to burn and some telegraph operators to be electrocuted. Another interesting history lesson stems from the events surrounding the nuclear tests of 1962 in the South Pacific, military code-named Starfish Prime. That test caused disruption in various electrical systems and knocked out the streetlights in Hawaii about 900 miles away as a result of the EMP generated by the nuclear blast.

People who forget their history are doomed to repeat the same mistakes. Many books and movies are available that detail past disasters, each of which has lessons to teach, and some of which have applications in other disaster scenarios.

YouTube has dozens of videos and documentaries online from various news broadcasting and private services that clearly demonstrate geomagnetic storms hitting earth on a fairly regular basis! The province of Quebec, Canada, was hit by a relatively small geomagnetic storm in 1989 that caused a cascading failure of the electrical grid, which in turn took down the power to a host of cities in the northeastern United States. In fact, smaller geomagnetic storms cause the aurora borealis, which is seen regularly in the northern latitudes, and was seen as far south as the Caribbean during the Carrington Event.

Even some of the disaster-survival movies out of Hollywood representing other potential disasters present some interesting scenarios and teach some survival methods that are worthy of consideration. An example of this would be the scene in the movie *The Road*, in which actor Viggo Mortensen uses a flare pistol to defend himself and his son from an attacker using a bow and arrow.

In the end, by compiling and studying materials on various kinds of potential and historical disasters, your intrinsic understanding of these things will grow over time. You can even share some of these materials with younger children—so long as you supply guidance.

Take Action Against an Ominous Threat

As mentioned, the most difficult disaster scenarios may be those that follow a major solar storm or HEMP attack that causes an irreversible collapse of the North American electrical grid. Such a collapse would lead to a catastrophic failure in the entire supplies and services infrastructure, resulting in millions of people violently competing for the few remaining resources. At this point, deadly force could very well be used both defensively and offensively.

But how can anyone come to grips with the concepts and methods entailed in lethal combat? The thought of having to kill others so that you can live gives rise to all kinds of philosophical, religious, and moral issues, to say the least.

Many people have been buying guns not only for themselves but for their children, under the theory that the kids will be able to engage in lethal combat to defend the family unit. I would like to strongly suggest that anyone who is considering arming children take some time to carefully consider a few sobering thoughts.

If you put firearms in the hands of your children, who may have to use those weapons in combat, then you had better be prepared to see your child shot dead or horribly wounded. When a hollow-point bullet enters the body, it initially makes a hole at the entrance wound approximately equal to the diameter of the bullet. As the bullet travels through the tissues and organs, it expands in diameter as it spins like a roto-tiller cutting and severing tissues and carving an increasingly larger hole. If the bullet hits bone, it shatters inside the body like a hand-grenade sending bullet fragments everywhere. If the hollow-point bullet exits the body intact, it blasts out a large chunk of flesh that is several times the diameter of the entrance wound. Furthermore, if the bullet was traveling at a velocity faster than the speed of sound when it enters, which many do, in addition to the damage already described, the shockwave will also do hydraulic damage to the tissues and organs as well, which in and of itself is very severe. Wounds like this are oftentimes fatal even under the care of skilled doctors in a highly equipped trauma hospital, especially when the relatively fragile bodies of children are involved.

Think carefully about that image and the impact that event would have on your family's morale as well as your own. Trust me, it's not like what you see on TV or in the movies. The blood and uncontrolled screaming and crying doesn't end when the movie ends or pause for a commercial break about coffee or new cars. This kind of visceral trauma and the subsequent loss of life hollows a person out to the core. In many cases, the survivors are left in a state of deep depression that severely handicaps objective thinking and tactics.

Conversely, if you are the one seriously injured or killed in the presence of your children during an actual firefight, any child combatant will likely lose focus and will probably end up dead as a result. It's hard enough for trained soldiers to ignore comrades who get hit during a firefight, let alone inexperienced civilians and children. So the concept of having a child "holding the line" if you go down is just ludicrous.

If you engage in a firefight, you stand a good chance of becoming a corpse. Even our most highly trained military operators, such as Navy Seals and Delta Forces, are killed in action on a regular basis by relatively untrained terrorist operators.

As you see, I hold strong opinions about paramilitary survival methods. I believe that if you fully understand the realities of these potential scenarios, you will formulate plans that avoid your family having to endure such horrors and choose another more reasonable path.

Speaking for myself, I couldn't stand living knowing that I got my wife or children killed by setting them up to engage in armed combat when there was a better, smarter option. For me, the universal maxim is *Combat should always be the absolute last resort.*

Taking to the Sea

If you, too, are inclined to avoid combat to preserve the safety of your loved ones and survive, the other option is to completely remove your family and friends from any and all threats. You can accomplish this by means of a large sailboat. When I speak of a "large sailboat," I mean a boat of at least 40 feet in length. However, I should note that boats as small as 26 feet in length have successfully circumnavigated the earth with only one person on board to operate and manage the boat. In this option, the mental preparations are somewhat different than sheltering in place or bunkering down, and the outlook is much better. That said, the idea of sailing away across the ocean to a remote island can be overwhelming. Having done it myself many times, I can say that it's the fear of the unknown that makes the concept daunting. There is good news though: Traveling by boat at sea is far safer than traveling in a car, and the process can be accomplished in small, easily achievable steps.

First, let's examine the perceived risks of the use of a sailboat, or any boat, as a bug-out and relocation platform.

According to the U.S. Department of Transportation report "Accidental Deaths—United States—2009," the annualized death rate attributable to car accidents is significantly higher than for boats; however, it is not a direct comparison because people spend more time in their cars. The ratio of car-related deaths is 1 out of 6,400 people. The death rate for the same period for boats is 1 out of 17,000 people.

As a result of the combination of the pirates off Somalia and popular movies such as *Pirates of the Caribbean*, piracy has received a considerable amount of media attention worldwide. Even though the media has sensationalized piracy beyond its true proportions, it is still a serious matter if you are planning on transiting the near-coastal waters off certain third-world countries. Statistics from 2012 regarding acts of piracy according to the International Chamber of Commerce (ICC) are as follows: 297 incidents worldwide with 150 of those incidents occurring within the near-coastal waters of Somalia, where "near-coastal" defines the waters adjacent to and within 200 miles of shore. The balance of the 147 acts of piracy were distributed along the near coastal waters in other areas of the world, including Africa, India, Asia, and South America. The data indicates there were no acts of piracy outside near-coastal waters, offshore on the high-seas, or at any of the islands in the Pacific and Atlantic basins.

ICC has a great online map depicting areas of piracy (www.icc-ccs.org). A quick study of that map and the statistics informs that vessels traveling far offshore are not attacked. Furthermore, if you avoid transiting near-coastal areas known for piracy, you greatly reduce your risk. Those areas are: Africa and the Red Sea (Somalia alone accounts for 50% of all acts of piracy worldwide), Southeast Asia, the Indian subcontinent, and Ecuador. These days, pirates use small, fast-moving powerboats so their range at sea is severely constrained by limited fuel capacity, ability to navigate beyond the sight of land, and offshore weather. As a result, the general rule is that pirates tend to stay well within 200 miles of their own coastlines and bases of operations. Pirates are also very limited in their ability to navigate offshore. The boats they use typically don't have any modern navigation systems and the vast majority of pirates cannot navigate using a sextant or modern means. The best strategy to avoid any run-ins with pirates is to avoid their areas of operations.

So as we see, the risk for mariners from sea monsters, rogue waves, hidden rocks, reefs, pirates, and other such events is much less than that of simply driving your family car to the mall.

The other consideration for most people embarking on long-range sailing expeditions is that of leaving family and friends behind. I admit this can be hard. That said, being homesick is totally survivable. The optimal situation is to bring as many family members and friends with you as your boat can reasonably accommodate. On a properly equipped boat, more people may be better, so long as everyone is carrying their own weight with chores and fishing.

Another consideration is that of physical health. Some people may not be healthy or physically fit enough to go to sea, although I have seen many couples in their 70s running large sailboats by themselves without any crew. In fact, my wife and I easily operated a 70-foot vessel by ourselves over the course of a four-year, 12,000-mile voyage, and we are in our late 50s. I would speculate that most people in average physical condition without any critical medical conditions would fare very well on a large sailboat. Sailboats at sea are very forgiving. Since they travel at a relatively slow speed, operational stresses are low, especially compared to driving a car. My family usually watches movies or play cards while we're under way!

The biggest single challenge for most people considering sailing for survival would be getting up to speed on nautical skills. In addition to learning the basic mechanics of the boat, considerable knowledge is required to operate and navigate the vessel across several thousand miles of sea and locate an ideal island or other landmass. However, you can learn these skills relatively quickly assuming you're willing to devote yourself to the project. Some of these same skills would also be required for any land-based survival approach.

The ocean is a big place, and relatively safe. Once a sailboat is beyond the horizon it is virtually impossible to find except by skilled operators using radar. Such operators who are already at sea will likely be in the same strategic position as you: looking to avoid any contacts. And once you have relocated to an ideal island for instance, with a thousand miles of water around you in every direction, the odds of any hostile entities reaching your position are for all intents and purposes nearly zero. Added to which, such a location is quite defensible, should you choose to stay, as opposed to the option of leaving for another location, which is easily effected when you have a sailboat.

The mental preparations for a nautical bug-out are achievable by almost anyone who is willing to put in a reasonable effort. These mental preparations are primarily equivalent to learning what is most often considered an exciting and fun hobby that is suitable for almost all ages. Even young children catch on fairly quickly. My son was fully capable of running a navigation watch aboard our

57-foot sailboat on his own by the time he was 12 years old, including navigating under radar in dense fog and at night.

Most people find that by the time they have spent a couple months sailing their boats locally, and put in some study time, their trepidation about going to sea is greatly diminished. With the confidence gained from actual experience aboard your own vessel, heading out to sea will probably seem more like embarking on an exciting adventure rather than a harrowing escape.

Anatomy of a Disaster

In order to develop a logical strategy for surviving various disasters, it's important to understand the general trends of various disasters, how they unfold, and the stages of any adverse event. Obviously, not all disasters start out in the same manner. Many disasters take an initial toll of lives at the onset, including hurricanes, tornadoes, earthquakes, tsunamis, nuclear and biochemical events, and pandemic diseases. In these events, an initial level of casualties occurs as a direct result of the initial impact. Other potential events, such as geomagnetic storms and HEMP attacks would have no direct physical effect upon biologic organisms. In these cases the casualties would likely result from secondary effects such as panic caused by the complete loss of technology and supply-chain infrastructure. Survivors may become dangerously violent as they compete for limited resources.

Most disaster scenarios posit widespread social unrest fueled by a serious lack of resources and violent competition for the remaining finite resources, including the most basic things like water, food, and fuel. The lack of resources would likely stem from the cascading catastrophic failure of our highly leveraged technological infrastructure. The loss of the national electrical grid is of paramount concern, since that adversely affects our entire critical infrastructure. Almost everything that runs on electricity will cease to function.

In late July 2012, when the large parts of India's electrical grid failed, the Associated Press reported the following:

> Electric crematoria were snuffed out with bodies inside, New Delhi's Metro shut down and hundreds of coal miners were trapped underground after three Indian electric grids collapsed in a cascade Tuesday, cutting power to 620 million people in the world's biggest blackout …. Hundreds of trains stalled across the country and traffic lights went out, causing widespread jams in New Delhi.

Fortunately this man-caused blackout only lasted several hours. If it had gone on for a few days or more, the country would have been thrown into a catastrophic crisis. The U.S. government has grown very concerned about the very real possibility of a catastrophic failure of the North American electrical grid caused by a severe geomagnetic storm or a terrorist attack on the U.S. using an electromagnetic pulse weapon. Either of these events would have essentially the same effect: the complete failure of the national electrical grid. A 2004 Congressional report entitled "Report of the Commission to Assess the Threat to the United States from Electromagnetic Pulse (EMP) Attack" describes the likely effects of such an event on the critical infrastructure of the United States. It's a real eye-opener to say the least. The bottom line is that we would suddenly find ourselves living in a situation more or less equivalent to the late 1800s. Some reports[6] on the loss of the electrical grid estimate that approximately 90 percent of all Americans would be dead within 12 to 18 months of such an event—that's up to 270,000,000 Americans dead within 18 months! These reports forecast that most deaths will stem from violent competition for resources and disease.

The good news is, there is a way to avoid being part of that statistic. The most important part is to be prepared.

A partial list of essential services that would immediately cease to exist without electricity includes the following:

Traffic lights   The ensuing accidents and permanent gridlock will turn streets and roads into impassable parking lots.

Fuel (pumps are powered by electricity)   Many vehicles will run out of gas on streets and roads, forming more roadblocks.

Refrigeration   Perishable food supplies and medicines will spoil.

Sewage systems   Public health hazards will result.

---

6   http://www.wnd.com/2012/08/emp-attack-90-of-americans-would-be-dead/

Water systems Drinking water will become scarce and valuable.

Streetlights Cities will be totally blacked out at night.

Food supply Because trucks will cease delivering food and other vital supplies, supermarkets and pharmacies will be cleaned out in a day or two.

Communications Telephone and Internet systems will fail. Emergency assistance from 911 will be unavailable. Banking and other commerce will cease.

Medical services Hospitals' emergency generators will run out of fuel in 72 hours or less.

A few of the longer-term issues include:

- Fuel refineries will go offline, so no fuel will be produced.
- Manufacturing industries will be offline.
- Nuclear power plants will go offline and could lose containment.
- Looting and plundering of infrastructure will render it useless and beyond repairable.
- Uncontrolled fires will break out and spread.
- Urban and rural guerilla warfare will continue until resources are totally depleted.
- Widespread disease will break out.

As these scenarios play out, competition for resources in the cities will turn into violent conflicts. Once those finite resources are gone—or even before—the masses from the cities will migrate outward in all directions. Hundreds of thousands of people, or more, will be on the move.

Many of these people will have already killed others to survive and will not hesitate to continue to do so. Most of these aggressive survivors will know there are people who have prepared and who have stockpiles of resources and are located both in- and outside urban areas. The infiltration of armed masses into rural areas will occur in this scenario, and it's only a matter of time. For the sake of their own immediate survival, these masses may divide up into smaller groups or "hoards" who will aggressively and intelligently seek out any survival facilities, hidden or otherwise. Sooner or later, most people who have bunkered up will probably be faced with these hoards, and lethal combat will ensue.

Examining a map of North America, one can quickly surmise that very few places will be free from this kind or problem. Some vehicles full of survivors will make it out of the cities and with a range of 400 to 500 miles, will deliver these, probably-armed, survivors far into rural areas, where they will take up defensive positions. Survivors on foot can easily cover 15 to 20 miles in a day, so in about three to four weeks many of these survivors will disperse from the cities in all directions to distances up to approximately 500 miles as well. However, the places that are remote enough to offer a better chance of survival are so far away that the odds of reaching them through the gridlock and asymmetrical warfare will be low. Talk about a gauntlet, this would be the mother of all gauntlets!

Make a Plan

Those who don't want to think about the realities of the world today and adopt a wait-and-see attitude, in a disaster will end up having to react to events as they occur. Sadly, their lack of planning will likely result in the deaths of themselves and their families.

The good news is there is a much easier path for those people who understand the realities of our world today, are willing to take reasonable steps, and make plans that are in proportion to the risks. Some unique survival paradigms can even provide a return on investment of time and money even in the event that they are not needed for survival. One such paradigm is the use of a sailboat as is outlined in this book.

It is essential that you make a plan (or plans) that include:

- The members of your family/group: number, ages, special needs, etc.
- Where you are headed.
- Where you will meet up and how long you will wait.
- What you'll need to take that isn't already on-board (a customized bug-out bag).

WHERE TO GO? SCENARIOS, STRATEGIES, AND TACTICS

In developing your personalized offshore survival plan, it will be up to you to identify and research your own offshore bug-out location. It wouldn't serve anyone's purposes if I were to suggest suitable locations—for obvious reasons. Also, the selection of such an "offshore" location is somewhat subjective and may be based upon personal living preferences. Some people don't mind the cold, so locations closer to the poles may not present any hardship. However, from my chair, locations at or near the equator present the best-case survival locations, for reasons that will become clear as you read further on.

When you examine the weather patterns and high altitude winds for the northern hemisphere, it's clear that in the event of a catastrophic nuclear disaster, such as conventional nuclear war, the majority of fallout will remain in the northern hemisphere. Another consideration with regard to nuclear events is that most of the potential targets are in the northern hemisphere, as are 90 percent of the world's nuclear reactors.

In the event of nuclear war, land masses in the northern hemisphere, including key agricultural lands, may be contaminated for many, many years. As bad if not worse is that most of the freshwater is contained in lakes, rivers, streams, and aquifers, and fallout would continue to affect those very limited quantities of freshwater. Compare those supplies to the vast quantity of water that is contained in the world's oceans and available on land in the southern hemisphere, and you begin to see a primary advantage to heading south by boat. The possibility of nuclear winter provides another advantage. It's no secret that surviving in cold weather involves hardships that mostly relate to maintaining your body temperature. Wood-burning stoves are essential for heating and cooking in cold-weather environments and that means a lot of hard work, constantly cutting, hauling and stockpiling wood from a diminishing supply. However, the planet will remain warmer around the equator, and year-round ambient survival temperatures will be more favorable for those survivors who take up residence in equatorial areas. And, although a nuclear winter would reduce the effectiveness of solar panels worldwide for a year or more, in equatorial areas they would have a better chance of functioning.

We have never experienced a nuclear winter; the best approximation of the effects of such an event would be the conditions experienced after eruptions of super volcanoes. One such event was the Mount Tambora eruption, in 1815, which sent so much dust into the upper atmosphere of the earth that it created what would arguably be the equivalent of a nuclear winter. It caused a distinct change in the world climate: In the spring of 1816 world temperatures cooled, and instead of the northern hemisphere warming as summer approached, the climate cooled. Widespread crop failures occurred, leading to food shortages and famine in Europe, the United States, and elsewhere.

So we see that for a variety of reasons, lands and islands near the equator and farther south are likely to be a better choice of destination than anywhere in the northern hemisphere. Many of these lands may remain viable for agriculture, and the seas should remain fruitful since the food chain is based on plankton and krill, which are in great abundance in the seas of the southern hemisphere. As an added bonus, observations over many decades have shown that hurricanes do not form within five degrees of latitude north or south of the equator. Therefore, islands that are located within 300 miles north or south of the equator are not subject to hurricanes, so weather-related issues are minimal.

By some estimates[7], there are approximately 45,000 tropical islands worldwide. Of those islands, it is estimated that 28,000 are at least 5 square hectares in size or larger. Generally speaking, an island provides a great base of operations for a sailboat. Many islands have sheltered lagoons or inlets where a boat can be safely moored long term. And since a sailboat also provides shelter and security, once you have arrived, your survival needs are as simple as just maintaining food and water supplies, and islands can also help with those tasks.

Most tropical islands receive a certain amount of rainfall from passing squalls. In addition, many tropical islands are made up of porous materials such as limestone and decomposing coral, so some of the rainwater ends up trapped in the rock. On coral atoll islands, as this rainwater percolates into the ground it settles into a lens-shaped layer that essentially floats on top of the denser seawater deeper underground. For centuries, natives of such islands have used very shallow wells to gather this freshwater, which though somewhat brackish is suitable for consumption. Islands with different geologic origins may still have aquifers that can be tapped via springs and streams. Resourceful survivors can utilize these naturally occurring sources of water to augment other methods such

---

7   http://en.wikipedia.org/wiki/Island

as rainwater catchments, and solar-powered seawater desalination stills or desalination plants (see Chapter 4).

The naturally occurring sources of food that are available on most tropical islands are largely related to the sea. Pelagic and reef fish are in abundance, as well as crustaceans, mollusks, and eatable seaweed, which can provide a long-term source of nutrition. Many islands also offer edible plants and fruits as well, which vary from island to island. Coconut palms are common and in addition to the fruit provide materials for manufacturing shelters and textiles. Additionally, the trees can be tapped to harvest a nutrient-rich sap containing essential minerals, which has been used by island people for centuries.

Research starts with detailed charts of the ocean in your potential theater of operations. If you live on the eastern seaboard of the United States, you probably won't choose to sail around Cape Horn and into the Pacific Ocean, even though that is quite possible. Therefore, you will likely be looking at locations in or near the Atlantic Ocean. The same holds true for sailing preppers on the West Coast, who will probably be most interested in destinations somewhere in the Pacific. The are also some very large lakes and rivers that might also provide some limited strategic or tactical survival advantage with the use of a boat, in which case obtaining and studying the detailed charts for those areas would be prudent.

The key is to do your research carefully and thoroughly. Once you find a primary destination, gather all the information you can, including detailed small-scale charts, and note the latitude and longitude on your navigational charts. Using the compass rose on the chart, you can determine the initial heading that you will steer when you bug out from the coast. You will want to do the same for a secondary, or backup, bug-out location.

A SAMPLE PLAN

Let's consider the following example. In the event of the worst-case scenario, such as the loss of the national energy grid, our party of four adults will be leaving from the West Coast of the United States and heading for one of several islands in the South Pacific. Our primary, "Plan A," destination island is approximately 4,300 nautical miles away, a distance that has been determined through researching the chart that covers the area between our departure point and destination. However, we will need to determine how much water, fuel, and supplies are required to reach our primary destination, and additionally, an added amount of these necessities that would allow us to easily reach areas in and around New Zealand (7,000 miles away) as our backup, "Plan B." And when we arrive at either destination, we want to have enough reserve food and water remaining to sustain us for four months so that we won't have to worry about that while we are getting established at the new location.

Therefore, our vessel needs to be properly equipped and provisioned to safely and comfortably deliver four people to any destination within 7,000 miles of its home port, plus have enough additional food, water, and basic infrastructure to allow for an additional four months at the selected location. I think we all realize there are closer locations that might offer a great long-term respite from any strife that would have necessitated such a voyage. However, we must always plan for the worst and hope for the best in these enterprises.

Basic Calculations for the Voyage

Using a 40- to 50-foot-class sailing vessel on a long voyage, I like to plan for the purposes of provisioning and equipment for an average speed under way of 5 knots. Note that this is not the same as the theoretical displacement speed (hull speed) of the example vessel—that would be greater than 5 knots. In other words, under ideal conditions this size vessel will travel considerably faster than 5 knots. However, we must take into consideration such things as counter currents, adverse wind and sea conditions, and other possible delays, like angling a large fish for an hour or two on occasion. If you use 5 knots as your planned speed under way in your calculations, you will most likely arrive on or ahead of schedule—and that's vital when it comes to your stock of consumables on a long voyage. Speed over the route of travel is important because it determines how long it will take us to cross the distances, and that in turn allows us to make the calculations regarding the supplies needed during the voyage.

So at 5 knots speed under way, we are planning on making an average of 120 nautical miles per day (24 hours ×5 knots). For the purposes of this example we want a total "endurance profile" (fuel, water, food, and supplies) adequate for a voyage of 7,000 miles, which as we see by doing the math is about 58 days at sea, if we travel nonstop. So we need to provision for 58 days plus another four months' reserve of supplies, which is a total of about 180 days for four adults. That's a lot of food, water, and fuel, and will take a good amount of effort and planning to have ready at a moment's notice. (See Chapter 4 for more on provisioning.)

BE SURE EVERYONE IS ONBOARD

If you have a family or are part of a prepper group, then any plan of action must be well known to each and every person in the family or group. To make certain that everyone clearly understands the plan of action, and implications of that plan—such as that anyone who doesn't follow the plan will be left behind—you will need to conduct family or group meetings and review those plans.

Having detailed printed copies, with a basic map, available for each person is important, because in situations involving potential panic and confusion, being able to refer to written instructions can be vital. Typing the plan of action on both sides of a sturdy business card, which fits well into any wallet or purse, is a handy idea, and you can also laminate it, making it waterproof.

Here is an example of what information such a card might contain:

1. Primary Meeting Location—Marina @ 24th St., slip 23
2. Secondary Meeting Location—HWY 101 bridge @ Green River
3. Primary Com Freq.; SSB 4.149.0 USB / CB—Ch 28 / VHF Ch 71

4. Secondary Com Freq.; SSB 2.082.5 USB/CB—Ch 34/
   VHF Ch 82
5. #1 Verification Code—Say "Igloo"; Correct
   response "Seaweed"
6. #2 Verification Code—Say "Viking"; Correct
   response "Zebra"
7. Code name for the group member: Mike Smith =
   "Africa"
8. A very basic map showing the primary and
   secondary meeting locations.

Through the use of the information on the emergency
card, group members can securely locate and/or communicate with the vessel and each other. During- and post-
emergency, the vessel should be standing by with all the
primary frequencies beginning at the onset of any disaster
and until either all the members arrive onboard or until
there is a coordinated frequency switch. Normally, by
using odd (less popular) frequencies for communications,
the frequencies will be clear. However, in the event there
is too much interference (intentional or otherwise), the
vessel or a group member can simply say, *Switch to secondary coms*, and once this action is confirmed (*"Roger"*) by
all members, then the communications "net" (vessel plus
all members) switches to the secondary set of frequencies.
This way, if someone is listening in, they have no idea of
what frequencies you have switched over to. If any party
of the group is concerned they may not be talking to the
right person (someone high-jacking the coms), a group
member can simply say to the person on the other end of
the communication, *Verify, I say "Igloo,"* and wait for the

response. Only someone in the group with a card will be able to give the correct response, which in this case is, *Seaweed*, and this ensures the security of the operation. You never want to use the same verification code twice on the same communications frequency, so the #2 Verification Code is for use in the event a member needs to make a second verification, or in the event you don't recognize a voice, or after a communications frequency shift, to make sure you are talking with a group member on the new frequency.

If the primary meeting location is blown for any reason, you can simply communicate with the group by saying, *Meeting at secondary location* and naming the time. This way you don't have to say the location "in the open" over the frequency, since all members of the group can simply refer to the card if they're foggy on any details.

As another part of developing such a plan, you will need to establish how long you will wait before the sailboat leaves port, and that may vary depending on the type of disaster (see Chapter 6). There are obvious scenarios where you could realistically allow up to a couple of days for everyone to arrive at the boat. These considerations may also be based on your specific situation and the geographic locations of family or group members at the moment a disaster strikes.

Therefore, you will need to establish a method for secure communications during disasters as a part of your plan of action, which would help everyone to reach the boat. In our hypothetical plan, we have two meeting locations. It makes sense to have regular disaster preparedness meetings with your group and review the set procedures that will be established for each possible disaster scenario, especially in regard to how long the vessel will wait at the primary location before it departs. Assuming everyone makes it in time to the primary location, the secondary location is a moot point. However, if for some reason the vessel is forced to depart from the primary meeting location, it must be established in the preparedness meetings exactly how long the vessel will wait at the secondary location, assuming everyone is operating in the blind as a result of loss of communications for whatever reason. This amounts to what may be termed a "default plan" that covers what your group will do if one or more people in the group, or the vessel, should lose all communications capacity.

Shortwave radios (SSB, Single Sideband Radio) are available in both large base-station units, such as would be used onboard a boat, as well as portable handheld units, and will communicate easily over hundreds of miles. VHF (Very High Frequency) radios, which operate on frequencies much higher than SSB radios, have a more limited effective range. Full-powered 20-watt base station units will provide solid two-way communications up 20 miles, and the lower-powered 5 to 6-watt handheld units are reliable over distances ranging from 5 to 20 miles depending on terrain. VHF radios may be used in place of SSB radios if your group is well within that localized range. Like all emergency communications gear, these radio units should be properly packaged and protected from damage and along with batteries that are checked and fully charged, packed in a shock-protected Faraday cage or box. Then they can be unpacked post-disaster and used to maintain communications with the group and the boat using a preselected frequency included in your written plan of action. This allows each member to check in with the boat and each other and provide a situation report (SITREP). Having coordinated team communications also allows for last-minute modifications of the plan of action in response to any unforeseen issues in a way that keeps everyone in the loop, thus assuring the ongoing viability of the plan.

In addition to meeting and discussing the plan of action with the entire family or group that makes up your sailboat crew, you should also conduct training drills at least once or twice a year. In the case of nautical prepping, the training drill can be part of the family or group's summer vacation—which is yet another benefit of this paradigm. This also allows the team to then spend time onboard using the equipment and systems and gain experience that will be fun. In the event of a disaster, it may also become the difference between life and death.

MAKE A LIST, AND CHECK IT TWICE

Once you have rehearsed your plans (ideally many times before the onset of any disaster) and worked all the bugs out, make a checklist of items that will need to be done at the onset of a disaster and list them in proper sequence as an addendum to your laminated emergency data cards. All the laminated data cards must be completed and distributed to all family/group members during "good times," well in advance of an event. In other words, in addition to the laminated data card with radio contact and location data, it might also make sense to provide a secondary personal card that is specific to each person in your survival group. It would be like a shopping list outlining things that each particular person would be assigned to bring along with them. Maybe one person has an extra medical kit, and another person has some extra binoculars, for example. Of course each person's list would also include the personal items they may require, such as special medications. As a commercial pilot, I have made hundreds of landings and takeoffs. Nonetheless, like all commercial pilots, I still use checklists for landings, take-offs, and emergencies to prevent anything from being overlooked. As discussed, I strongly suggest that you make and use some form of a checklist once you have established your plans. Family/group members should be instructed to keep their emergency data cards with them at all times!

SAFETY TRAINING

As a part of this planning process, it's important to arrange for everyone in your family/group to obtain some initial training in first aid and CPR. Regardless of whether or not you end up onboard a boat cruising the seven seas (or the local lake) as a part of a survival strategy, or just for fun, having these basic skills is a must for everyone.

In my book, CPR and first aid training and certification are must-have skills for both adults and children, no exceptions. This allows everyone the comfort of knowing that anyone in the group can render these lifesaving services. And it's surprising how children will rise to the occasion if given the chance. Prior to embarking on our first sailing expedition, my wife and our two children (then eight and eleven years old) all took an advanced first-aid CPR certification class that was given by a paramedic from our local fire department. The class was very well received by both daughter and son. Classes are given at hundreds of locations all over the country and some of them are free of charge.

A proper first aid and medicine kit is also an absolute requirement onboard. Schedule a sit-down consultation with your family physician. You may have individuals in your family with specific medical or pharmaceutical needs, and those needs will need to be addressed long-term. Your doctor is best equipped to make the recommendations and provide the types and quantities of drugs and supplies that should be in your medical kit. Trust me—you need a lot more than a box of bandages and antibiotic ointment. Be honest with your doctor and inform him of your survival plans and needs, and he should be able to provide you with a medical kit up to the task. Normally, the physicians I have met are very helpful when it comes to assisting with providing the proper medical supplies for a boat heading offshore long-term. If not, then find another doctor who understands your needs and who will assist you in your preps.

There are a few things that may be in an advanced medical kit that will require some training if you are to use them safely. Things like sutures and injectable drugs all require a doctor's prescription and some basic skills. For instance, some injectable drugs are for intramuscular use only, and should those drugs be introduced into the vascular system, serious side effects may occur. Therefore, you must learn how to perform various injections and as such, you should consult with your doctor as to the use of these materials and the need for possible training for emergency use.

CHAPTER 2
Choose the Right Boat

If you are considering a boat for the peace of mind it might provide as a means of shelter and escape from some potential disaster, there are a number of interrelated considerations you need to consider. Among them are cost (your budget); boat size, type, and what it's made from; and whether to buy a used boat or have one designed and built to your specifications.

This chapter offers a broad overview of these factors to get you started with the process, as well as brief descriptions of what's involved with having an existing vessel retrofitted for your needs and of the design-and-build process. This chapter is not meant to be exhaustive—you will need to do much more research and consult with experts before you can acquire a boat—but it should provide enough to get your thoughts organized.

A thorough discussion of boat anatomy for beginners is outside the scope of this book. For more information, on page 66 you'll find a list of books that will give you a solid introduction into how various types of vessels operate.

What Will It Cost?

Cost is a big issue for most people. If you are thinking about having a boat designed and built to your specifications, the question of total cost cannot be addressed until the design has been fairly well defined. As a result, there may be some back and forth between your wish list and the final design, and even then you should plan for cost overruns. Building a boat is not unlike building (or remodeling) a house: It always costs more than you want it to, or think it will, but in the end it's worth spending the money to get what you want, or in this case, will need to survive.

BUY OR BUILD?

Having said that, there are ways to save money, one of which is to find a well-built, used recreational or commercial boat that already has all the basics, and then tweak it to your needs. You can save about 50 to 70 percent of the cost of a new vessel by doing this, but you will need to proceed very carefully. Unless you are yourself expert enough to know what you are doing, I urge you to hire a qualified maritime consultant to help; it is well worth the cost. (See "Adapting a Used Boat" later in this chapter for more on this topic.)

Of course, in buying a used boat you are exchanging control for economy. It usually means accepting several compromises in the layout or function. By contrast, having a boat designed and built exactly to meet your needs may be the best way to achieve the right combination of form and function.

Whether you buy or build from scratch, your goal should be a boat that feels like home—a place where you and your family and friends want to be. Your collective morale will depend on that, and morale makes the difference between success and (possibly fatal) failure.

If you cannot find an existing new or used boat that fills the bill, but creating a totally new design seems daunting, you may be able find what you need from an existing stock design offered by yacht architects, who these days typically have portfolios you can peruse on the Web. So you may discover that finding a suitable existing design can save quite a bit of time as well as the cost involved in developing a new design.

Another factor to keep in mind is the (typical) 10 percent commission paid to the yacht broker when you buy an existing boat. The cost of an entirely new design is ordinarily less than the commission on a comparable boat.

If this seems unlikely, you can submit a design brief to a boat designer of your choice and request an estimate. Then compare that estimate to the 10 percent broker's commission you know is already built in to the price when shopping for an existing boat.

How Much Boat Do We Need?

Setting questions of cost aside for a moment, my first rule of thumb for an expedition vessel is **Bigger Is Better**. Larger vessels are more sea-kindly (ride better in heavy seas) and provide more privacy and more space for equipment and supplies. By the time you add all the systems and creature comforts that will make your boat suitable to the intended task—which is surviving in comfort—a boat that initially seemed large will have shrunk by quite a bit. So you want to start with as much as you can afford.

This leads me to my second rule: **Form Follows Budget**. The boat must be large enough to comfortably accommodate you and your family or friends (crew) without anyone having to sleep on a table or the like. Each person should have a dedicated berth and a place for their clothing and personal items. (See "Layout Considerations" later in this chapter, for more on this topic.)

The ideal boat must also be large enough to carry sufficient supplies for everyone onboard for several months, including enough (rationed) freshwater for a minimum of one month, with the means to make and/or collect additional water to augment this supply. (Chapter 4 goes into more detail about necessary and desirable equipment and provisions.)

The good news here is that generations of cruising sailors have lived at sea for months—or even years—at a time. It is entirely doable, with no great hardship. The logistics of going to sea in one's own boat have been worked out and tested many times over by many people on many different types of boats.

Many designers have attempted to assign a certain length or tonnage per person for comfort or livability. While many generalizations can be made, the specifics of your own particular requirements override all such preconceptions.

Of course, equipping a large vessel can be an expensive proposition if you want all the bells and whistles. I'm not suggesting that a smaller boat cannot do the job, far from it. For example, a pocket cruiser is a smaller vessel—25 to 30 feet long—that is specifically built for heavy offshore use by one or two people. And if that's your entire crew, then a pocket cruiser may work just fine for you.

I am just saying that if you want happier people over the long term, lots of creature comforts go a long way. Freshwater showers (heated as needed), better-quality food, laundry services, entertainment (books, movies, and music), and so forth will make living on a larger boat similar to living in a condo.

By contrast, expedition sailing on a smaller vessel requires more sacrifices by the crew, because you are forced to make do with a lot less. In survival mode, having less as opposed to more, is a consideration that you must make with great care. Some people cannot endure the hardships that a small vessel can impose on a long voyage—so bigger is better.

That said, in my opinion, compared to an underground bunker, even life on a small sailboat would be heaven.

What Material Is Best?

Unless you're planning to limit your travels to inland waters, lakes and rivers, the boat must be truly seaworthy. Seaworthiness is characterized by the quality of *survivability*.

Survivability means that the boat must be strong enough to weather the elements. It must have sufficient stability to withstand being knocked down by wave and wind. It must behave well at sea and have good directional stability. It must have sufficient performance to stay out of trouble. And while doing all of this it must also be able to *keep the water out!* For this, the boat's strength is critically important.

Most of those characteristics are a function of the boat's design and construction. The last, however, depends more on what it is made of. So let's look first at the different materials used to make boats and how they respectively do the job of keeping the boat dry inside and therefore *afloat*.

WOOD AND FIBERGLASS

Fiberglass and wood are less-than-optimal choices for an expedition vessel due to those materials' vulnerability to heavy impacts because they lack elasticity, especially compared to metal.

A fiberglass boat can be designed and built to have enormous strength. Purely on strength-to-weight basis, fiberglass can even compare favorably with aluminum. However, conquering the tendency of a composite structure to abruptly fail on heavy impact is extremely difficult. I think it is safe to say that few if any of the fiberglass boats on the market will have been built with this criterion foremost in the mind of the designer or builder.

It is possible to build a composite boat using Kevlar with vinyl ester or epoxy resins in the laminate. With these, one can quite literally create a bulletproof hull. With proper design, the result will be a far more resilient structure that is better able to resist impact than a typical composite of glass fiber and polyester resin. But even so, the result will not be as elastic as a metal structure.

Further, neither fiberglass nor wood is fireproof or at all abrasion resistant.

FERRO-CEMENT

Once popular for amateur boat construction, ferro-cement—which is constructed very much like an in-ground swimming pool, using a plasticized concrete that encases steel re-bar—has fallen out of favor, primarily due to the enormous amount of labor and advanced skills required to achieve a good result. Done well, it can produce a workable structure that is quite strong, but it will be enormously heavy when compared to other materials.

Because of its construction, ferro-cement—layers of cement laid over a steel mesh framework, which is also called an "armature," has extremely low tensile strength and little elasticity. Although the steel mesh underlying the cement is somewhat flexible, that does you little good when the cement simply disintegrates on impact. The armature alone can do nothing to keep the water out.

Cement is also not fireproof. Remember the World Trade Center?

ALUMINUM

Aluminum is superior to fiberglass, wood, or ferro-cement. It might be a viable option for an expedition boat. In fact, considered on the basis of strength per unit of mass, aluminum is very strong and flexible—it is actually stronger than steel! In other words, if you were to build an aluminum boat and a steel boat to the same design and with equal weights, the aluminum boat would have considerably greater strength.

As a practical matter, when designing a boat for construction in aluminum, the sizes of the structural members will be approximately 1½ times that of the equivalent member in steel to bring the aluminum structure up to the same overall strength as the equivalent steel structure. However, since aluminum is about ⅓ lighter than steel per unit of volume, the resulting aluminum structure will weigh roughly 30 percent less than the same structure in steel, with equivalent strength.

For an ultimate survival craft, though, aluminum has a number of disadvantages:

- It loses approximately ¼ to ⅓ of its strength when welded, although this can usually be compensated for by good design and by reinforcement locally.
- It is relatively easily abraded by reefs, rocks, waves, etc.
- It is subject to fatigue failure to a much greater degree than steel. That is, it becomes increasingly brittle under stress or impacts, (again, reefs, rocks, waves, etc.).
- It is very active galvanically—it is both a good conductor of electricity and prone to corrosion. Therefore close attention must be paid to isolate the aluminum from other metals (to prevent corrosion) and to carefully design and then closely monitor the vessel's electrical system.
- It is not fireproof. The magnesium in the alloy, if ignited in a sustained hot fire, will burn freely.

STEEL

I can say without reservation that, on the basis of strength and survivability, steel is the best choice as a structural material for an ocean-voyaging boat. While strength is its key characteristic, steel is also highly resilient—it will absorb incredible impacts before failing. Steel can be bent and deformed radically and permanently without rupture.

On a boat, this property of elasticity is an essential requirement for keeping the water out. A material that can absorb impact without failure is vastly superior to other materials that do not possess this ability.

Steel is also extremely abrasion resistant. For these reasons, steel "wins" as the material of choice for our survival craft. While other materials may have certain advantages, when you're considering a boat for the purposes anticipated by this book, nearly all of them quickly fade into the background.

A story may help illustrate this point. Many years ago, I observed the steel yacht *Joshua,* which had been washed ashore during the infamous Cabo San Lucas storm of 1982. The yacht had landed on top of a few fiberglass boats that were already on the beach, destroying them completely, and was subsequently landed upon by another fiberglass boat, which was also destroyed in the process.

Afterward, the owner, a well-known yachtsman named Bernard Moitessier, was so distraught that he sold the boat to a couple of beach bums from Port Townsend, Washington, for a dollar.

The new owners shoveled out the sand from the inside, and then hired a bulldozer to push the boat back into the water. They then proceeded to salvage the gear, rigging, and sails off of other destroyed boats and sailed *Joshua* up the West Coast to Puget Sound.

When I saw the boat hauled out in Port Townsend, there was a giant dent in her side at and below the waterline made by the lead keel of a sailboat pounding on her in the surf. The divot was big enough that if plated over it would have been able to hide a small family. But the vessel did not leak. She had done her job to keep the water out.

Boat Types

The type of boat you choose will depend on your budget, your physical ability, and your seamanship skills. If you're planning to retreat to a large lake or river, less skill and equipment will be needed and a suitably sized vessel of nearly any type might be a reasonable choice.

However as the body of water increases in size, so must the vessel's inherent survivability, to accommodate extremes of wind and waves, and for the sake of maximum autonomy from shore-based support systems.

If you're equal to the task of voyaging offshore, and you have chosen a vessel that is capable of doing so, you can quite realistically relocate to a distant location, whether the vessel is propelled only by an engine, sails alone, or both.

The design considerations for voyaging under power are essentially the same as those for voyaging under sail. Either vessel type must have a robust structure, a seaworthy arrangement above and below decks, a sea-kindly shape, and adequate stability to withstand the effects of wind and waves.

SAILBOATS

Looking back at my own experiences of voyaging on the ocean, the most rewarding have been accomplished entirely under sail without an engine onboard. (For that matter, they were accomplished without an electrical system or any fancy electronics!) By studying the ocean currents and wind patterns, one can go just about anywhere on the briny deep using only the sails. To have accomplished such a voyage is its own reward.

For the purposes outlined in this book, I believe a sailboat is the most fuel efficient and reliable choice for voyages of any distance—whether coastal or offshore.

MOTORSAILING BOATS

If you need a motor anyway, would a vessel optimized for both sailing and motoring modes of propulsion be the best choice? Many people think that a motor sailing boat will neither motor nor sail very efficiently, and will offer examples showing that they are at best only 50 percent capable under power and 50 percent capable under sail to prove their point.

Certainly it's true that a poorly designed vessel will prove their point. However, it is possible to build a motorsailer that is 100 percent capable as a sailing vessel while also being 100 percent capable as a motor vessel. Appendix B (page 177) gives some examples of good motorsailers.

MONOHULLS VS. MULTIHULLS

The debate between advocates of monohulls and multihulls is a longstanding one. It is not my intention to get into that debate here. In fact, I have a place in my heart for both types, and when used for the ideal application, each design has its advantages.

In addition to extensive experience with monohull vessels, in the 1980s, when I lived in Hawaii, I operated a 52-foot sailing trimaran (three hulls) as a charter boat that provided sailing and diving trips to the nearby islands. A decade later, I operated a very large aluminum cruising catamaran (two hulls) in the Pacific Ocean. The boat was 70 feet long on deck by 32 feet wide and weighed 45 tons. Even though the boat was ketch-rigged for sailing (mainmast and a mizzen mast), it also had two diesel engines capable of powering the boat at 9 knots over the water. The boat was spacious and could easily accommodate 16 people onboard without a problem.

Such a vessel can provide an outstanding survival platform, and because it can enter waters as shallow as 4 feet deep, it offers you a wider choice of potential harbors. We sailed that boat thousands of miles, had a lot of good times, and to this day I still have many friends that I met while serving as the captain of that boat.

Nonetheless, I still prefer monohulled boats over multihulls for blue-water sailing, although each has advantages and disadvantages.

Here is a summary of the primary trade-offs:

Living space Generally speaking, for a given length on deck, cruising multihulls will have more room inside than monohulls of the same length, whether power or sail. On the other hand, monohulled boats of proper design can offer almost as much room.

Draft   Shallow draft boats, including large cruising catamarans and trimarans can navigate shallow areas of water without becoming grounded. Oceangoing monohulls are limited to navigation in deeper waters, and therefore cannot access many locations.

Ride   In my experience, multihull boats are less sea-kindly than monohulls. A monohull vessel is heavier, and a heavy boat is not pushed around by the action of the sea as much as a lighter boat. Conversely, a multihull tends to pitch sharply when heading into the waves and to roll abruptly when waves come from the side. The motion tends to wear on the crew, and fatigue can become a problem on longer passages with seas larger than 2 meters. On the catamaran I operated, we had great difficulty moving around the boat in larger seas. This was no fault of the design but rather a typical characteristic of a multihull vessel.

Stability   Multihulls have enormous stability under most conditions; however, in very rough seas it is possible for a boat to tilt beyond 90 degrees. If that happens in a multihull, it flips, and the game is over, because they are just as stable upside down as upright. A monohull (sailboat), on the other hand, will tend to right itself. The weight of the keel places the boat's center of gravity below the waterline, so the vessel wants to remain upright.

Some boat designers, including Michael Kasten, have come up with solutions to the last issue with multihull vessels. Visit www.kastenmarine.com if you are interested in more information on these innovative crafts.

POWER BOATS

In some locations and some disaster scenarios, a power boat may be a viable bug-out option. For example, if you live on the Great Lakes, a power boat could be a better choice than a sailboat for fleeing to Canada.

A motor yacht will usually have a shallower *draft* (less hull and keel below the waterline) than a sailboat, allowing a broader range of travel in shallow water. Motor vessels are usually also wider and taller than sailboats. Thus, size for size, the accommodation space of a motor yacht will usually be greater than that of a sailboat. Appendix C (page 183) shows some examples of well-proportioned power boats.

Layout Considerations

The layout of your boat is quite important to consider. Some requirements are related to how the boat will be used (e.g., destination) and others are a function of personal preferences. And one can affect the other, but for now let's look at them separately.

BELOW DECKS

In basic terms, the security of the crew involves more than mere "survival"—it also involves creating a sense of being "at home" in your own space, engendering a sense of well-being.

During offshore voyages it quickly becomes obvious that, like an army, a boat's crew marches on its stomach. In other words, the crew must be well fed. For this, the galley must be fully functional in design, well-equipped, safe, and easy-to-use in all conditions, including heavy weather. There must also be a space dedicated to socializing, whether for meals, reading, doing projects, or just hanging out. This is all an integral part of good design and will go a long way to assuring your crew's morale stays good.

Sufficient rest is also important and will be assured by comfortable berths for everyone. Each crew member must have a dedicated bunk (bed) where he or she will have ample space to sleep. All bunks must be long and wide enough that an average adult can sleep comfortably. A single bunk should be at least 24 inches wide and 74 inches long. This is not a standard mattress size, however. On the last two cruising sailboats I built, we designed the bunks to accept off-the-shelf mattresses, as opposed to using cut-to-size foam cushions. Each bunk should be equipped with an LED reading light and a small 12-volt fan. Built-in shoulder boards (also called lee boards) or another form of restraint system to keep people in their bunks during heavy weather is also needed.

Provide all of this and you'll have addressed the morale factor right up front.

Let's look at some general layout examples. First, say you are equipping a 50-foot oceangoing motorsailer that has a single cabin for two in the stern of the boat and another cabin for two in the bow, each with a bathroom, or *head,* with a toilet and shower. This is a fairly common layout and provides a good amount of privacy. Our vessel also has a full galley and dedicated seating-dining area in the *saloon,* a living area off the galley with a large table and seating all around.

Another option would be to have two or three cabins, all located in the forward section of the boat. In this example, all of the private quarters are in very close proximity, which limits personal privacy even when there are doors on those cabins. A lack of personal privacy is of concern since it always affects morale.

SUPERSTRUCTURE

The design of the superstructure (if any) is another consideration. If you plan to seek shelter somewhere on a large inland body of water, then things like an inside steering station (*pilothouse*) may be less critical than if you are considering traveling offshore, where a pilothouse is invaluable.

If your boat will have a superstructure, regardless of layout, it should be modest by comparison to the boat's size. It is not a good idea to cram an enormous superstructure onto a relatively small boat, because you wind up with a short, fat, top-heavy boat, and this configuration is not conducive to ultimate survival at sea. It gives the boat a very large windage area and often not enough below the water.

If we use Beebe's A/B ratio limitation as a rough guide, there should be no more than twice the profile area above the water than the profile area below the water. The vast majority of motor yachts these days exceed that ratio, which may be another reason to avoid buying one.

A large superstructure is also unfavorable in terms of comfort at sea; you don't want to place the crew too far from the axis of roll—too high up. And of course, large superstructures are structurally much more vulnerable.

Short, fat boats with high superstructures mainly need robust dock lines, and not much else because, frankly, that is what they are designed for: sitting at the dock!

In summary, the larger the superstructure, the greater the windage, which is very unfavorable with regard to stability in high winds and detrimental to sailing performance. It is much better to have a modestly sized pilot house, possibly extending into a modestly sized deck house aft.

Adapting a Used Boat

If you decide to have a boat designed and built, you will do so with the knowledge of your expected crew capacity and it will be suitable for your plans and needs. However, if you acquire a vessel second-hand, you must take care in that selection process. Some boat brokers have very little or no offshore cruising experience. In my opinion, these people should not be relied upon in any way for selecting a boat because many of them are little more than salesmen, though they may talk a good game, and might even have some weekend sailing experience.

For example, never let anyone convince you that a table or seating area can become a suitable sleeping area for crew or passengers on a cruising vessel. That's just wrong, for a host of reasons. Some recreational boat manufacturers build in tables and seating areas that convert into bunks so they can claim the vessel accommodates more people than there are bunks. In my opinion, vessels like this are manifestly unsuitable for extended offshore use.

The best-case scenario may be to find a good used commercial boat that it is already equipped with good-quality commercial gear, which is a big bonus to such an acquisition. Chapter 4 discusses important equipment you will need on your vessel. Be sure to read it before you buy a used boat!

HIRE AN EXPERT—OR THREE

As I suggested earlier, you will need to proceed very carefully unless you know your way around boats. If you don't have experience, hiring a qualified maritime consultant is well worth the cost—and by "qualified" I mean someone with actual experience who understands all the systems and has used them in an expedition paradigm. With understanding that's based on actual survival experience and the demands on the boat and the equipment, that person will be able to guide you in the successful modification of any used vessel into a worthy survival platform.

Once you think you've located a suitable boat, the next step is to have it surveyed. Make sure to hire the surveyor yourself and that he or she is certified and has a long list of references. The best surveyors are also U.S. Coast Guard–licensed masters and are therefore experienced vessel captains. Some certified surveyors are not licensed ship captains, but they are less likely to bring the perspective of what makes a vessel suitable and ready for open sea. Conversely, even though most experienced captains can easily do a great job of surveying a vessel and making it ready for going to sea, insurance companies require that a certified surveyor do the survey. So my best advice is to find a highly experienced captain who is also a certified surveyor.

Then make sure the surveyor knows that you are heading far offshore and that the boat needs to be up to the task. With this instruction, a fully qualified surveyor will make a lot of recommendations. This shouldn't be alarming unless the recommendations stem from some major structural defect or issue.

You should also hire a qualified mechanic to survey the engine and transmission on the boat, as well as any generators. Most surveyors are not fully qualified to perform an engine and transmission survey.

REPAIRS AND UPGRADES

Once the vessel survey is completed, you will have a list of recommendations from the surveyor and the mechanic. Normally, at this point some negotiations on price may take place; for example, the seller may offer a discount to cover the costs of some previously unknown defects. You will want to find a certified mechanic and electrician to meet with you and the surveyor to go over the survey, devise a plan, and determine the cost of completing all the recommended repairs mentioned in the vessel survey.

Normally, any survey of a used boat will need to be done while the boat is out of the water, as this facilitates close inspection of many parts of the boat, including the hull, rudder, propeller, drive shaft, and associated fittings. Some repairs and upgrades may also have to be completed while the boat is out of the water, so get those done first.

Before heading offshore, you will want all new zincs and all new cutlass bearings, wherever they are located, in addition to replacing or repairing any other worn or defective parts. "Zincs" are simply solid pieces (or plates) of zinc metal that are attached to the hull and all metal parts that are below the waterline. These protect the boat from electrolysis, which can damage any vessel. Cutlass bearings are used in underwater applications where you need to support a rotating shaft, such as a propeller or rudder shaft and it consists of a special rubber material that lines the inside wall of a bronze or fiberglass tube. The rotating metal shaft fits snugly in the tube and rides against the rubber material that is lubricated by water, given that the entire assembly operates underwater.

One type of part to consider replacing, whether or not they are worn, are any plastic valves. Never use a plastic valve anywhere near or below the waterline of a boat. In fact, I don't like plastic valves anywhere on my boats because they have a habit of failing at critical moments. Bronze valves are typically used on wooden and fiberglass hulls, and stainless steel ball valves (316 or 321 grade) on steel hulls, although you can use stainless steel ball valves on wood or fiberglass hulls as well.

If You Want to Start from Scratch

If you have the means, a boat built to your specifications will provide the best survival platform for you and your family or friends. If you plan on a long-distance bug out, you will probably choose either a sailboat or motorsailer, constructed of steel, or possibly aluminum. The details of the process are beyond the scope of this book and would vary to some degree depending on the boat designer or naval architect you choose to work with, as well as the specifics of your requirements. For more information on the process of designing and building your own vessel, visit Michael Kasten's website, www.kastenmarine.com, where he specializes in prepper naval architecture.

CHAPTER 3
Test Your Platform

Acquiring a suitable sailboat is exciting and affords the opportunity for a lot of fun. However, it is also a lot of work in the beginning. You, as the captain, need to become familiar with your new vessel inside and out. Unless you are an experienced sailor already, you will need to take classes to become certified. And the other members of your family or group also must become comfortable aboard the boat and need to learn their roles and responsibilities as crew. This includes kids.

Most children love boats of all kinds and can't wait to start messing around onboard. I believe in encouraging them to participate in all functions combined with education. Some sailing schools will allow children if accompanied by parents, so everyone can share in the education. Other times, budget allowing, you can hire a sailing instructor to come aboard and teach sailing skills and practices onboard your own boat, and in this case, the children also benefit from this hands-on education, a solution that I personally recommend. On a sailboat, once educated and trained on the equipment, children can be effective crewmembers in many areas of operations once at 8 to 10 years of age. Starting them as early as possible with the activities onboard that are most interesting to them is the best way to proceed. Their interests will grow and expand as they observe you and the instructors that you bring into your project.

Get to Know Your Boat

To become acquainted with your new boat you need to start from the keel up—and I mean that literally. If you had your vessel custom built to your specs, then you are probably already well acquainted with it, and that gives you a head start. If you bought a used vessel, then you should have participated in every aspect of the pre-purchase vessel survey, where a marine surveyor goes over every inch of the boat and makes a detailed "buyer's report" of all his or her observations and recommendations (see "Hire an Expert—or Three" on page 54). During this process, you can learn a lot from a good surveyor by asking lots of questions. Remember that there are no dumb questions.

The following sections lay out the steps you should take to acquaint yourself with a used boat and make sure it is seaworthy. If you had your boat custom built, then these steps will be less critical. However, you and your key crew should still go over every inch of the inside of your vessel, including the bilges, to familiarize yourselves with everything.

CLEAN AND PAINT

With a used vessel, the next phase of learning your boat is achieved by cleaning every inch of her, top to bottom. Do this before the mechanic and electrician start their work inside the boat and *do it yourself,* with the assistance of your key crew. This chore gives you an intimate knowledge of your new boat, as it will have you peering into every space and crevice on the boat, cleaning and painting where needed. It also allows you to make a used boat look and smell like a new one.

You will also likely be cleaning your engine and transmission and this is also important: It gives you intimate knowledge of every part on the exterior of the engine. This process should be combined with a detailed review of the engine and transmission manuals, noting the names of the various parts of the engine and transmission as well as all the points of service for oil, lube, filters, zincs (if any), and impellor pumps.

SCRUB THE BILGES

Once you have the engine and transmission cleaned and painted to look like new, clean the bilge under the engine and transmission so that it's completely free of any oil or debris and is dry. In many boats the bilge area under the engine space is the lowest place in the bilge, so water that gets into the boat accumulates there. The engine bilge will probably have a bilge pump or two, and you will want to make sure that any such pumps are in like-new condition and their water intakes and float switches (which turn the pump on) are free of any debris or obstructions.

Keeping the bilges in the boat clean and free of any debris is critical to the proper functioning of the bilge pumps. (Some technicians seem the think that bilge areas are garbage cans and allow all kinds of junk to fall into the bilges. If you see any technician on your boat allowing anything to fall into and stay in the bilge, I suggest that you remove that person from your service immediately, as that is a sign of poor workmanship. A good technician will clean up his area before he leaves each day, even if the job is not yet complete.) If a bilge pump becomes obstructed by some junk, the pump may not function properly when it is needed to dewater the boat—if you have a leak or other issue with water coming in—and that's not a good thing. Failed bilge pumps have caused boats to sink, and even tiny objects such as wire trim or a toothpick can jam the impellor and cause the pump to fail.

Once you've dealt with the bilge under the engine space, continue on and scrub all the bilge areas in the boat so that they are dry and clean. You need a clean, dry bilge so that you can notice and deal immediately with any leaks, whether from incoming water from a leak in the hull or the engine (fuel, coolant, or oil) or transmission. A clean bilge allows you to immediately identify the liquid by its color and/or smell: Coolant is usually green. Engine oil is black. Transmission fluid is usually red. Diesel fuel is sometimes dyed red but it smells different than transmission fluid. Some coolants and transmission fluids may have other characteristic colors, so it pays to familiarize yourself with the colors and smells of the various fluids used in your particular vessel's systems. That way, once you identify a leaking substance in the bilge, you are better equipped to find the source of the leak and repair it before it causes a problem such as a burned-out transmission or overheated engine. I paint my bilges white so that anything and everything shows.

CHECK THE VALVES

When you're down in the bilges you will notice several through-hull valves that allow water from outside the boat to come into the boat as a part of the boat's water intake system (for engine cooling, sanitation, etc.) or to exit the boat (bilge pumps, sanitation). Carefully note the exact location of each of these valves on a permanent diagram that is kept in a handy location in the boat—if you need to shut off one of these valves in an emergency, you don't want to fumble around trying to find the handle. Also, make sure that all these valves open and close smoothly. It's a good idea to "exercise" them by opening and closing all the valves a couple of times a year. Some of these valves have places for lubrication and they should be lubed with the proper marine-bearing grease, which is the kind that is used on boat-trailer wheel bearings, where such bearings are exposed to water.

LEARN YOUR ENGINE

The next step in getting to know your new boat (new or used) is to have your chosen mechanic come to the vessel and perform a complete engine service in your presence. Explain to the mechanic that you are headed offshore for an extended period and won't have access to a mechanic, and need a crash course on servicing your own engine. You will have to pay extra, since explaining the process will take far longer than simply servicing the engine, but it's money well spent.

If the mechanic balks or seems uncomfortable with your request, find another mechanic. A good mechanic will not have any problem with this request, as long as you are covering the cost of his extra time to teach you.

Assuming you are starting out with a sound used engine and transmission, or new units, here are the basic skills related to hourly service intervals that you will need before heading offshore. (Note that these skills also apply to any engines that drive generators.)

- How to change the oil and filters on the engine and possibly the transmission (many transmissions have no filter).

- How to change out the fuel filters and bleed all the air from the fuel injection system.

- How to diagnose a failed fuel injector, change out the bad fuel injector, and bleed the fuel system.

- Where all the engine zinc anodes (sacrificial metal anodes used to protect the engine and other metal parts from electrolysis) are located and how to change them.

- How to service any impellor pumps on the engine, including checking and replacing the rubber impellor before failure.

- How to clean all seawater intake screens.

- How to adjust the valves ("the overhead") on the engine. This is usually done only after hundreds of hours of engine time on most engines, but if you're at sea for a very long time, and run the engine a lot of the time (say to power a diesel

generator) you may hit the hourly service interval
for the value adjustment.

- How to change out the engine accessories, including the starter, alternator, and water pump. Here
again, these items are normally reliable for hundreds of hours of use—or on commercial engines
thousands of hours. So this knowledge may not be
needed—unless it is.
- Where the engine thermostat is located and how
to change it.

Once you have learned all of the foregoing, you will
want to start a detailed maintenance log, recording the exact engine hour reading off the Hobbs Meter in the log for
each maintenance item performed along with the time (in
hours) when the next service is due. You can find hourly
maintenance recommendations in the manufacturer service manuals. If your engines don't have Hobbs Meters
but the tachometer shows engine hours, you can use that
hourly time. Otherwise, have Hobbs Meters installed.

Maintaining the engine and transmission this way will
ensure both maximum reliability from your systems and
that you don't accidentally overlook anything.

READY STORAGE AREAS

At this point, your boat should be absolutely clean and
dry everywhere on the inside. This includes all the cupboard and storage areas in the boat. This is the best time
to make all storage areas ready for provisions.

First, using a large commercial salt shaker—like the
aluminum ones used in pizza kitchens for pepper and

salt—apply a very fine dusting of boric acid to the bottoms of all storage areas and all areas in the bilge that are above areas that could potentially get wet. When I say a fine dusting, I mean that it should be barely visible to the eye. The purpose of this is to prevent infestations of cockroaches, a common problem on boats. If you get cockroaches after you lay in all your provisions, it's a huge chore to clean everything out to dust with boric acid. By taking this step now, you ensure that your boat will remain free of these serious pests for a long time to come. Boric acid is deadly to cockroaches, yet is relatively harmless and non-toxic in all other respects.

Once you have carefully dusted all cupboards, storage areas, crevices, cracks, and other dry locations that are not in the open, you are ready for the next step. Before laying in stores, line the bottoms of all shelves and storage compartments with textured rubber matting. In areas where space isn't critical, I like to use ½-inch perforated rubber commercial kitchen floor mats. In areas where you can't use that thick a mat, there are much thinner rubber mats you can use. The key is that they have ventilation—holes that allow air to flow through and under the matting.

Once you have your matting picked out, you can cut it to fit exactly into cupboards and storage areas. These rubber mats also keep stored goods from sliding around when the boat is at sea and keep the boric acid dust underneath viable. At this point, the storage areas and cupboards are ready for stores.

Seamanship and Learning the Ropes

If you are new to sailing, your journey toward self-sufficiency as a sailor should start with some study of the traditional books. If you are an "old salt" who has already owned a boat for some time, some or all of the remainder of this chapter will be review.

There are hundreds of books about sailing, seamanship, and navigation, but about a half-dozen are considered time-honored references by many mariners and are the core text books at many maritime academies. The following books cover (with a bit of overlap) all the important basics; I recommend you start by acquiring and studying them:

Chapman Piloting and Seamanship

Dutton's Nautical Navigation, by Thomas J. Cutler

American Practical Navigator, by Nathaniel Bowditch, LL.D.–Published by the U.S. Navy Hydrographic Office. (This old book may be out of print, but is very interesting and available in used copies and is also available online at: ftp://ftp.flaterco.com/xtide/Bowditch.pdf)

World Cruising Routes, by Jimmy Cornell

The Ship's Medicine Chest and Medical Aid at Sea, U.S. Government Printing Office–DDHS Publication No. (PHS) 84-2024–Revised 1987. (A newer version is also available online at: http://www.fas.org/irp/doddir/milmed/ships.pdf)

The Nautical Almanac, U.S. Naval Observatory. The *Almanac* is used in conjunction with a sextant for celestial navigation. Note that you must have the current version if you want to be able to use the moon and planets for navigation. Otherwise, with some corrections, as explained in the *Almanac,* you can use an older version for navigation using the sun and stars.

After you have spent some time reviewing the aforementioned books, you will be ready to make the most of some basic sailing lessons. At this point you have a couple of options.

You can join a local sailing club and start out by sailing the smaller, easy-to-manage crafts or you can have a qualified instructor come aboard your vessel and give you private lessons, specific to your boat.

There is value in learning to sail a dinghy or other light sailboats; however, if you have a good instructor and you're a quick study, you can be sailing your own boat after a half a dozen lessons or so. It's not that complicated once you get into it, and as I have said, even kids catch on quickly. Initially, it can be akin to learning to drive a car with a manual transmission.

Once you have your basic sailing skills down pat, you understand the navigational rules for traffic and signals, and you've earned your basic sailing certification, you can start sailing. Start out with day sails with your family/crew, building your experience and confidence over time and in varying wind and sea conditions.

As time goes on, you can graduate to longer day sails offshore, returning before dark. And once you are comfortable, make an overnight trip, returning the following day. I suggest that on the first and possibly the second overnight trip you bring an instructor who has nighttime sailing experience so you won't feel stressed. This will allow you to gain experience without getting in over your head, since the instructor will know how to challenge you without asking more than you can handle, and is there to back you up.

It is important to keep in mind that many people get seasick—even experienced sailors. Especially before off-shore trips, I find it effective to start taking anti-nausea medication the night before I leave port. One natural medicine that is very effective is ginger, and I can buy ginger capsules at almost any health-food store. Start taking the ginger several hours before you head out. Another trick that can work well is to anchor out the night before leaving on the trip. This allows time for people to acclimate to the motion in steps. The motion of the boat at anchor is light, and when the greater motion of being under way occurs, people have adjusted.

During training sails—day or night—you can also put all the onboard systems to the test. In the course of these trips you will be running all your electronics, engine, generator, and more. In due course any irregularities will surface and can be easily dealt with.

As you extend your offshore experience, you will get to a point where you will be ready to travel to a nearby location and anchor out for several days to a week at a time. This will enable you to test the sufficiency of your power generation and energy storage systems—wind, solar, generators, and batteries—under actual use. In these tests, I suggest that you simulate at-sea operations by having everything turned on, including all the radios, radar, running lights, inside lights, refrigerator, freezer, autopilot, the works! And run all this stuff 24/7 to see how the charging and storage systems hold up. This test will let you assess the suitability of the capacity of your charging and storage systems so that you can upgrade as needed to be totally self-sufficient in the area of energy. If you find you have to run your generator too much, based upon your fuel budget and planning, then you'll need to add more solar panels and possibly a second windmill (see Chapter 4). With those upgrades, you may also need to add batteries to increase your storage capacity and take advantage of the added charging capacity. A qualified electrician can guide you in this very important process. Once you get your boat dialed in, it will become a totally self-sustaining habitat and bug-out vessel. In fact, you may even find, as we have, that it's just like a waterfront condo!

At this point, you will be ready for a more intense drill, in which you take your boat to a relatively secluded area and live aboard without leaving it for at least a week at a time. This will help to simulate being at sea in terms of being confined to the boat and learning to live with only what you have onboard. This exercise will also lead to the discovery of items you feel you cannot live without, which you can then add to the boat. This exercise will also be essential in creating your provisioning lists, where you establish your use of provisions over time, based on the people being served onboard. You then use this list or table to calculate the amount of supplies needed for a long voyage.

After spending a week confined to the boat, you will have some idea of what a long passage at sea will be like, although without the occasional challenges of the wind and seas and sailing in varied conditions, which takes a lot of the boredom out of a long passage. During the course of these various trials, you can also be working on your fishing skills, which can add a lot of quality food to the ship's supplies.

CHAPTER 4
Equipment Onboard Your Boat

In this book, I use the term *expedition vessel* to refer to any boat robust enough to handle the challenges of continuous long-range offshore use and supporting the people onboard for months or even years at a time. An expedition vessel is what is required to first allow people to escape any coastal area and then provide a relocation platform and shelter for long-term survival at remote, inaccessible overseas locations, far from any post-apocalyptic chaos.

Equipping your chosen boat can be challenging; you need to start with a plan and stick to it. If you are having a boat built for your specific needs, then the designer and builder may be able to assist you with equipping your vessel to some extent. This may be the best path for you, assuming the process is overseen by a consultant who specializes in maritime survival paradigms, such as expedition sailing. Some people, however, prefer to have a hand in the process, and doing so can pay off in terms of understanding and maintaining the vessel's equipment and systems in remote destinations.

Equipment and systems will vary greatly from boat to boat depending on several criteria, including the size of the vessel, number of people onboard, geographic area of operations, desired endurance profile, and level of creature comforts. How much equipment you actually need for physical survival may be less of an issue than what you can't "live without." If you consider the conditions on sailing vessels for the many centuries before the advent of modern technology, it's clear that, in a pinch, you can sail anywhere in the world with very little beyond the basics and a solid, seaworthy sailboat. By "basics" I mean things like water and food for the anticipated voyage, adequate clothing and footwear, charts, lead line, sextant, almanac, clock, compass, basic tools and supplies to maintain the vessel, extra sails and repair items, shore boat, spare anchors, anchor chain and rode, spare lines, lanterns and kerosene, kerosene stove, foul weather gear, a life jacket and safety harness for each person, emergency raft (made for offshore use), spare oars, a ships bell, and so forth.

For hundreds of years sailors made regular voyages over very long distances, even circumnavigating the globe, without the assistance of any of our modern technologies. This fact suggests that should all the modern equipment on your boat somehow fail, you can always fall back on time-honored knowledge and equipment to reach your destination. For this reason, I carry all the old-school technologies onboard the boats I skipper, including paper charts, wet compass, sextant, kerosene, lanterns, and so forth. This basic toolset would allow us to continue without modern electronics after an HEMP event or catastrophic failure of the electrical system (although much of the communications and navigation equipment will still continue to function in the wake of an HEMP attack or geomagnetic storm; see "Large-Scale Continental or Global Disasters" in Chapter 6). In addition to the basic equipment and systems for the operation of the vessel—including the equipment required by most state and federal laws—there is a long list of optional equipment that can be found on some modern expedition vessels. My preference is for redundancy in some or all equipment, so that you have a backup in case of malfunction or failure.

Once you have found a good used boat or are building one and are getting ready to buy equipment, keep in mind that your own life and your family's may literally depend on that gear. From my chair, there are two kinds of equipment: recreational grade and commercial grade. Most sailboat boats that are capable of offshore use are used only a few times a year, maybe totaling two to three weeks of usage per year, therefore some manufacturers offer less-expensive equipment that is suited to such light use. Conversely, commercial-grade equipment is made to be used all day, every day by commercial fishing fleets, commercial charter boats, tug boats, and so on. Of course, the cost is in line with that level of durability and reliability. But it's worth it.

In preparing for an event where the equipment may make the difference between life and death, you do not want to try to save money. (You can you can save money in other ways that won't put your life at risk.) Commercial marine electronics and equipment are designed to take a beating, and that's exactly what you want.

Also, if you have already decided that you will be using a boat, you can begin to acquire some of the needed equipment, especially personal gear such as: snorkeling gear, rain gear, fishing gear, charts, books, sextant, hand tools, and basically anything that doesn't need to be "installed" on the boat, or which may not exist on any used boat that you may buy.

Safety Equipment

Each vessel, depending on the type, size, scope of operations, and number of persons onboard will require various types and quantities of safety gear. The U.S. Coast Guard goes to great trouble to exactly define what safety equipment is required by law for your particular vessel. Additionally, there may be state laws that also require a specific complement of safety gear for your specific boat. Notwithstanding the state and federal safety gear that's required for your boat's size, type, and number of people onboard, here is a very basic list of what you need:

Lifejackets Ensure you have properly fitted lifejackets for "offshore" usage for everyone onboard. Keep in mind that one size does NOT fit all. You should attach a personal satellite locator (AIS—Automatic Identification System), whistle, and a strobe light to each life jacket. If possible, I try to also attach a waterproof handheld signal rocket (red flare).

Fire extinguishers   Keep an ample number of approved types of fire extinguishers and other fire-fighting
equipment for your type and size of vessel onboard.

Emergency signaling devices   This includes day and
night signals such as smoke, handheld and rocket/pistol
flares, water marker dyes, mirrors, whistle, trumpet or air
horn, bell, several oil lanterns with colored shades (red,
green, amber, clear), flashlights (waterproof LED lights
are best), strobe lights, radio transceivers (SSB, VHF, CB),
emergency satellite location beacon for the vessel, and a
strobe light mounted to the mast.

Safety harnesses   Be sure to have one for everyone
onboard. These are worn when personnel are out on deck
and are used to secure people to the boat so that they cannot be lost overboard. The safety harness has very sturdy
line that connects from the harness to a jackline using a
carabineer (a stout line that runs along the deck all the
way from the bow of the boat to the stern of the boat).
Using this system, the carabineer will simply slide along
the jackline as a person walks along the deck.

Life raft   Every vessel should have onboard a life
raft that is U.S. Coast Guard approved and certified for
offshore use for your vessel and the number of people
you have (maximum) onboard your boat. All approved
life rafts have some survival gear packed inside that is
accessible when the raft is deployed. However, I advise
that, along with the life raft and its minimal survival kit,
you should also have a waterproof ditch-bag (rafting
outfitters have such waterproof gear bags) ready to go

with the life raft, which should contain an additional complement of survival gear, including: signaling devices to the maximum extent possible (see above), food (MREs are OK), water (start with a gallon and reuse the container) *plus* we carry a hand-powered desalination pump, which provides an endless source of pure water in any event using any source of water (salt or fresh), fishing kit (100 yards of 30-pound test monofilament so you can make more than one rig, assorted feather and metal jigs, assorted weighted hooks so you can use fish scraps as bait, plastic hook remover, plastic hand-line reel, gloves), solar blankets (can be also used for additional shade and to collect and funnel rain water into the reuseable gallon water jug), handheld plastic compass, and two waterproof LED flashlights. Also bring a small first-aid kit (smaller version of the ship's kit) that also includes a tube of zinc oxide cream, wound closures, polysporin cream, analgesics, vitamins, chewing gum, small tube of super-glue, 3-feet of surgical tubing (tourniquet can also be used as a shock-line when fishing), seasick medication (we like ginger capsules), waterproof surgical tape, sterile gauze pads, compression bandage, assorted waterproof adhesive bandages, small curved sail-repair sewing needles, 20 feet of paracord (multistranded line used for parachutes; small threads can be removed and used as suture material with the curved sewing needle), a quality stainless steel multitool with knife and needle-nose pliers (needle-nose can be used for suturing).

First-aid medical kit   For the purposes of the concepts and ideas this book encompasses, coupled with the need for a quality first-aid kit for any vessel, it makes sense to have a comprehensive medical kit onboard. This kit is not a box of bandages and some iodine—it should contain the works! Items and supplies that are more frequently used therein should be in good supply (not just one box of assorted waterproof Band-Aids, but three!). I strongly advise meeting with your family physician or a doctor who has experience treating patients in a trauma ward and obtaining a list (and prescriptions) of supplies pursuant to your doctor's advice for your particular needs. There are a host of prescription drugs that you will also need (such as Tamiflu) and those will require a doctor's prescription. Be candid and explain what you are doing as far as prepping. A reasonable doctor will provide solutions for reasonable requests. In addition to those medical supplies, some people who require the regular use of prescription medicines will require supplemental quantities in the event of a long-term situation and your family doctor can help with those needs as well.

I strongly advise all mariners to carefully review all the up-to-date materials available at the U.S. Coast Guard's boating safety website: http://www.uscgboating.org.

Last but not least, the U.S.C.G. Auxiliary provides free-of-charge vessel safety inspections. I highly recommend that before setting out on your boat for any reason that you have them perform a safety inspection. This way, if there are any safety defects, you can find out about them and have them addressed.

Figure Out What You Need

Every boat designer, builder, captain, and owner has his or her own methods and logic, based on individual experience, for equipping a given vessel. As described below, several variables come into play, but as a rule of thumb, for expedition and survival missions, more is better than less, and a bigger boat can accommodate more. In determining what equipment you should have on your vessel, there is a lot to consider. The following sections discuss some very basic considerations.

HOW MANY PEOPLE WILL BE ONBOARD?

All things being equal, I like to start with the basic question: How many people will live onboard? The number of people being served and the vessel that has been selected determines what basic equipment will be required aboard the finished vessel as well as the optional equipment that you can reasonably install and carry. (Of course, the number of people in your party may also affect your choice of vessel.)

Keep in mind that successful cruising—especially cruising for survival—is all about making people feel as comfortable as possible within the limitations of the vessel. The health and well-being of the passengers and crew helps ensure the well-being of the vessel, and vice versa. In many ways, it's truly a symbiotic relationship between the crew and the boat. Quality of living, therefore, is an important consideration.

Of course water, food, and fuel are of paramount importance. If you have a generator, for instance, total fuel capacity affects how much power your generator can provide and for how long (solar and wind power are great but have some limitations).

Additionally, the number of crew on the vessel will help determine how a sailboat is rigged. Some variations of sail plans, standing, and running rigging will require more work, and with fewer crew, this might place too much workload on too few people.

WHERE AND HOW FAR ARE YOU GOING?

How far and where you intend to go determines several things, including the desired capacity of built-in tanks for fuel and freshwater, as well as how many provisions you will need. And given that sailboats have unlimited range under sail, we must nonetheless remain prudent and take into consideration any potential fuel needs, including near-term and future fuel needs, given that fuel may possibly become unavailable for a host of reasons. Extended endurance at sea and at remote locations requires more freshwater and fuel.

Operations in a colder climate will make heating equipment highly desirable or even a necessity. Conversely, in tropical climates, an air conditioning system (with dehumidifier) might be desirable.

If you are relocating for an extended period, you might want resources and equipment onboard that can be removed at your destination and used to establish an onshore base and area for habitation. This could require extra radios, radar, solar panels, batteries, and tools so that the boat still functions after you have set up your new land-based home. Additionally, you would want equipment and supplies for building a suitable long-term mooring system for the vessel (extra chain, anchors, buoy, shackles, etc.).

HOW MUCH SPACE DO YOU HAVE?

On smaller vessels, space restrictions can pose real challenges to storage and providing crew comforts. Realistically, however, with any size of vessel at some point you will need to find a compromise between "want" and "must have." Start with an ample wish list, and then pare it down to what actually fits onboard. This process will help prepare your crew for the realities of their new life—wherever that may be.

In the rest of this chapter I discuss equipment and supplies in terms of my own hands-on experience of 30 years along with that of other professional mariners. Do not listen to salespeople in marine supply stores. In most cases, they will just sell you what they have to sell, regardless of your needs. Also, in most cases, they have little or no real commercial operations experience, and the same goes for survival or expedition sailing experience. That said, when acquiring equipment, my advice is to buy the best equipment, electronics, and tools you can afford; it may have to last a very long time!

General Equipment

ANCHOR WINCH AND GROUND TACKLE

Your options in an anchor winch are hydraulic, electric, and manual. In my opinion, the best type is an open-spool hydraulic unit where the anchor chain is carried and deployed from the winch spool on deck, since stowing wet, dirty chain below decks is problematic. The openings that allow the chain to be stowed below deck can allow water to enter the boat, combined with the fact that the chain can be coated with mud and/or a myriad of microscopic marine organisms, which will begin to stink when they dry. Hydraulic anchor winches can be powered by either the main engine running a clutched hydraulic pump or by a backup hydraulic power pack run by the generator.

Hydraulic winches allow you to run the anchor chain in and out as much as needed without the disadvantages of electric winches, such as drain on the batteries and the potential for electrical corrosion, leading to reliability issues. Hydraulic motors last longer than electric motors in this type of service.

Manual winches are usually reliable but can be exhausting to the crew and have the additional disadvantage of being very slow in retrieving the ground tackle (chain and anchor).

As far as ground tackle goes, you should buy the biggest Bruce anchor you can fit on the bow of the boat, and connect it to as much Acco G-4 high-test chain as will fit on your winch. The proper size of anchor (weight) and size of chain (link diameter) is determined by the weight of the vessel and its size, which affects windage (how hard the wind can push against the boat). I recommend a minimum length of 250 feet of chain available on the winch and ready to deploy. I also recommend using an oversized swivel and shackles to connect the anchor chain to the anchor and the bitter end of the chain to the center of the winch spool. So, if you are using ½-inch chain, then you would be using ⅝-inch shackles and swivels.

All swivels and shackles should be American made and secured with red Loctite threadlocker, and the ends of the shackle pins flattened or bent over using a hammer so they cannot back out. (Trust me, when you want to remove them, they will come out easier than you would think.) Also plan on carrying at least one complete backup set of ground tackle (that means another big anchor and a lot of chain to go with it), as well as several spare shackles, a large inflatable ball fender (large enough to float the weight of 75 feet of chain), and a couple of extra anchors as well. This extra gear (anchors, chain, and float) will allow you to build a permanent mooring for your boat at your destination, so your ship's ground tackle is still available when you take the boat out.

DINGHY HOIST

Here again, your options are hydraulic, manual, and electric, and the same arguments apply as for the anchor winch. Hydraulic is best. I currently carry three backup electric winches because they fail about once a year in daily use. (I will be converting our current electric dinghy winch to hydraulic as soon as I finish writing this book!)

PARAVANES

Also called stabilizers or "flopper stoppers," paravanes help keep the boat from rolling back and forth in the trough of waves when there is not enough wind to use the mainsail to stabilize the boat. These stabilizers are made of galvanized steel or lead-weighted aluminum and look like small delta-winged fighter jet aircrafts. They are very simple to use, reliable, and are very cost-effective compared to some other types of vessel stabilizer systems.

DECK LIGHTING

For both forward and aft deck lighting, halogen is the brightest, so if you have the power for it (see below), stick with that. LED (light-emitting diode) lighting is dimmer but has the big advantage of using much less power.

Power Equipment

Power-generating equipment aboard your vessel will include the main propulsion engine by way of its alternator, plus any or all of the following: generator(s), solar array, and windmill. This equipment supplies electricity to charge the batteries, which (along with the generator) directly power the boat's navigation and communication equipment, lighting, sanitation equipment, appliances, tools, and so forth.

This means that the demands for electrical power from these combined systems can at times be nearly continuous when under way. These systems may utilize either 12 VDC or 120 VAC or a combination of both when under way or at anchor.

Because most of the equipment on a boat will be interdependent with regard to power sources, establishing the total potential power requirement, total energy production, and energy storage parameters is an important consideration and is best left to an experienced marine electrician working in close consultation with someone who has extensive expedition experience. Trust me on this: The system dynamics of long-term offshore use are much different than those of short-term or intermittent use, which is the only experience many qualified technicians have.

One important principle to remember is that although power demand is more intermittent at sea than on land, all the demands add up. Though you might not need electricity 24 hours a day, your electric-powered equipment may include a clothes washer and dryer, anchor winch, bilge pumps, water maker, sanitation, dishwasher, garbage disposal, microwave oven, entertainment systems, cabin cooling fans, air conditioning, heating, cooking (some vessel operators prefer to use electric or diesel stoves for heating and cooking rather than propane for reasons of both safety and availability), and electric tools.

There is a bit of a design balancing act between the size of solar array, windmill, and generator (the total charging system) and the size of battery bank (the storage system). Since sailboats use their main engines infrequently, it's best to leave the alternator out of the base performance calculations, although the alternator should be able to charge the system in a reasonable time if needed. For instance, if the solar array makes more power than the battery bank can store, that's not optimal. Conversely, if the battery bank will accept and store more power than the solar array can produce, the charging system can be augmented by the generator if there is no more room on the overhead for solar panels and a generator is being used daily anyway.

Because this topic is so extensive, it transcends the intent and scope of this book. The following sections simply provide an overview of the various power systems and give an idea of how they relate to one another. Some specific equipment recommendations are provided, but this is mostly intended as food for thought.

ENGINES

Most modern diesel engines are vulnerable to EMP because they have electronic fuel injection and associated sensors. Neither of these is acceptable in a survival or expedition vessel. Engines onboard the vessel that provide the main auxiliary propulsion and all power generators (see below) should be naturally aspirated diesel engines. The best engines for survival and expedition vessels have mechanical fuel injection and can be started by hand or by compressed air starter. Large, high-output alternators on the main propulsion engine will allow some energy to be recovered and stored in the battery bank (see "Battery System," below).

FUEL SYSTEM

On our current vessel, our generator uses about 0.6 gallons per hour. Since we can travel over unlimited distances using sail power alone, and the boat's tanks hold a total of 1,500 gallons of diesel, we can run our generator four hours a day for about 625 days under optimum conditions. Of course, if we use the main engine for close-quarters navigation and maneuvering, over time that would reduce the total available fuel for use with the generator.

However, even having enough fuel to last a year and a half should be adequate. If the government reports on the potential collapse of the North American electrical grid are reasonably accurate and the population is reduced to carrying capacity 12 months post-disaster, then many expatriate survivors should be able to return home to the United States after a year, in the worst-case scenario.

Obviously, it's important to keep your vessel fueled with clean, quality fuel at all times. However, that's not always as easy as it sounds, especially if you have to refuel under suboptimal conditions. Nonetheless, there are some key steps and equipment that will help prevent you having problems with fuel.

First off, you'll want to make sure your boat has Racor (Parker Hannifin) marine water separator/fuel filter housings and filters. I strongly recommend the dual systems with a selector handle that allow you to quickly switch from one filter system (fuel housing and filter) to the other. This enables you to service a filter that has plugged up while still using the other unit. Racor systems come plumbed and ready to install as a dual-unit setup.

If you purchase a new main engine for your boat, ask the manufacturer for recommendations on the proper size (flow rate) of Racor system for your engine. If you have acquired a used boat, or are repowering a boat with a used engine, then check with your local qualified marine diesel mechanic on the proper dual Racor system. Generators and outboard motors should be fitted with Racor fuel filter systems as well. Don't rely on the tiny inline paper or sintered bronze filters. Use Racor filters only!

The fuel in your tanks and that is stored on the boat must be properly treated so that it will not deteriorate in the tanks. Diesel fuel can be treated with additives that will prevent any growth of algae, which can sometimes form in some diesel fuel if it's left untreated. Also, moisture can sometimes find its way into fuel tanks. It's best to keep fuel tanks full so that condensation is eliminated as a source of water in the fuel. Diesel fuel can lose potency over time as its cetane levels can drop (cetane is analogous to octane in gasoline). You can eliminate this by using quality diesel fuel treatments that will inhibit the deterioration process as well as boost the cetane level of the fuel. Many fuel docks sell these additives. However, I would recommend checking the engine manufacturer's documentation (print or online) first, if possible. Alternatively, once you have a good working relationship with a qualified diesel mechanic, ask for a recommendation on fuel treatments and additives.

And all of the preceding goes for any gasoline you may store onboard your boat. I use a product called STA-BIL in my stored gasoline with great success. I have actually stored gasoline for more than a year in plastic jugs and then used it in my Honda outboard motor without any issue.

FUEL TRANSFER PUMP

A fuel transfer pump is another piece of equipment that's good to have if you need to move fuel from shore or from another boat to your boat. Make sure it's a high-volume pump made for fuel and runs on 12 volts. I carry 200 feet of ¾-inch fuel hose as well. If it uses an impellor, make sure you have extra impellors made from nitrile rubber.

AUXILIARY GENERATOR

I like having two generators (in addition to solar and wind power; see "Alternative Energy Sources," below). Naturally aspirated diesel is best, with mechanical fuel injection, although a gasoline-powered generator is also an option.

On our current vessel we have an 8-kilowatt diesel-powered electric generator, which we usually run for just a couple of hours a day. During the two-hour period when we are making electricity, usually in the evening before dinner, we try to use the full output of the generator by performing many tasks simultaneously: laundry, making water, cooking, charging the battery bank, heating water, cooling and dehumidifying the boat, running the dive compressor, and so on. We also try to plan any projects that require electrical tools for that same period.

We use as much power as possible when the generator is running because most industrial diesel generators use almost the same amount of fuel at full power output as with a partial load, since they run at the rated RPM as soon as they are started. This way we get the most utility out of every drop of diesel fuel used.

Ideally, when choosing a diesel generator, it should be a true industrial type, capable of running continuously for days at a time, if needed, even though in most cases you will run it for only a few hours per day, in accordance with your fuel-use planning. (Fuel-use planning projects how much power can be reasonably made from the generator on a daily basis and for how long, or as needed to augment solar and wind power to charge batteries while simultaneously accomplishing other power-hungry projects.)

There may be demand for power from both direct current (DC, battery) and alternating current (AC, standard electric) sources onboard the vessel simultaneously and at different times. Consequently, a reliable diesel generator is an important asset if the space is available. You should buy and install the largest primary diesel generator you can afford and have space and fuel for. Several companies make quality units, which is what is needed. Here again, your primary generator is the workhorse, so it has to be super-reliable. Cummins makes great generators.

You can augment the main generator with a smaller, cheaper portable diesel or gasoline unit. I found a great little 4.5-kilowatt portable diesel generator that can be started by hand or electrically. It will run my welders as well, so I can still use one if my main generator is down for repairs.

Personally, I don't recommend gasoline-powered generators as a primary onboard generator. However, they are fine as portable generators for use onshore or as an emergency backup when a primary generator fails. Honda makes a great little 2-kilowatt unit that is light, quiet, and relatively reliable. The only drawback is that its use could deplete fuel available for the outboard motor on your dinghy.

ALTERNATIVE ENERGY SOURCES

Solar Panels and Charging System

How much area can be made available for a securely platformed solar array—and therefore how much power that array can produce—depends on the size of your particular vessel.

Solar arrays must be securely and permanently mounted and capable of withstanding winds up to 100 knots or more. In many cases, this will require engineering an overhead platform of suitable size and strength. Most of the leading companies' solar panels are similar in quality and price. Buy the better panels; they last longer. Kyocera, BP panels seem to hold up well.

You will also need a solar regulator, and good ones are totally watertight. However, they aren't cheap!

Wind Generator

A wind generator can be added to almost any vessel and will provide additional power whenever there is adequate wind. Like the solar array, it should be mounted securely per the manufacturer's recommendations. The nice thing about wind generators is that they will produce power at night as long as there is adequate wind, and that power can be stored in high-capacity batteries for immediate or later use.

Primus Windpower makes small-frame, high-output windmills. I have a 400-watt wind-generator that I have been testing in actual use for six years now—and I mean it has been running continuously for that time. It has seen winds over 90 knots and still works perfectly. It has a built-in regulator. You can learn more by visiting their website at www.primuswindpower.com/index.php/wind-power-products.

BATTERY SYSTEM

Alternators

As mentioned, high-output alternators can be added to the boat's main engine so that whenever the engine is run it provides added power to the battery system. On some engines it's even possible to mount a second alternator so you can have two units making electricity at the same time. If space on the engine is small, this strategy allows two smaller units to provide the same kind of output as a much larger alternator with the added benefit of redundancy. I recommend Leece-Neville alternators, which are made for industrial, military, and commercial use.

Battery Bank

The number and size of batteries that are contained in your battery bank will determine how many amp-hours of power will be available for use. A vessel's onboard deep-cycle battery bank is critically important, thus the quality of the storage cells in the battery bank is of *paramount* importance, since they have to last a very, very long time under very heavy usage. When the sun goes down and solar panels have zero output, if the wind is not powering the wind generator and the diesel generator is offline, you are drawing all of your power needs from the ship's battery bank.

The difference in batteries is much more than meets the eye. A quality deep-cycle battery costs about three times more than a heavy-duty truck battery, but it is well worth what you get in return. It is a monumental mistake to try to save money by purchasing cheaper batteries (or any mission-critical equipment for that matter). When a cheaper battery fails prematurely, you can find yourself in a really bad situation. Quality deep-cycle batteries are nearly impossible to find in many foreign countries and it is a lot of work to replace them due to their size and weight.

Only two or three companies in the world make proper deep-cycle extended-use batteries in my opinion; two of those companies are Deka Batteries (www.dekabatteries.com) and Trojan Battery Company (www.trojanbattery.com). These very special batteries are much denser (same physical size, but weigh more) than standard truck or golf cart batteries because the lead plates in the cells are larger and more robust. This makes them extremely reliable over the long haul. In the vessels I have owned and operated using these batteries, I have seen an average lifespan of 7 to 10 years in hard use at sea under actual extended off-grid conditions.

Due to weight considerations, the battery bank must be located and properly secured in a space that can handle the weight, doesn't affect the vessel's trim (this can be a consideration in smaller vessels), has easy access for servicing (periodically adding distilled water), and is well ventilated. Batteries produce hydrogen gas, which can explode if it accumulates and then is exposed to a spark.

All batteries on any boat must be contained in U.S. Coast Guard–approved, acid-proof battery boxes, unless they are certified by the manufacturer as approved for use without a battery box (some batteries meet USCG standards for use without a battery box).

Battery Charger

If you have a large battery bank, it's important to also have a large capacity, high-output, marine-grade battery charger online between the diesel generator and the battery bank. A large-capacity battery charger will recharge the batteries much faster than a small-capacity charger, and that's important because you are burning diesel while the generator is running.

When it comes to anything electrical, I like having two of everything online and ready to use, including battery chargers. On our current vessel, we have two 120-volt AC (VAC) battery chargers, each making 80 amps at 12 volts DC. When both units are on, they have the capacity to deliver up to 160 amps.

Inverter System

An inverter system converts 12-volt DC to 120-volt AC—allowing your standard electric appliances and gadgets to run off energy that is stored in your DC battery bank.

Here you'll want some redundancy. I use one Xantrex 2,500-watt (continuous duty) main unit for some kitchen appliances. I also have a spare backup inverter unit of the same wattage (still new in the box). Our current ship has one 400-watt inverter for each cabin on the boat. They are installed in an array near to a dedicated main battery bank, and the 120 VAC lines from each dedicated inverter run to the specified cabin and are wired to GFI sockets in the cabins. In a pinch, any of these inverters can run one kitchen appliance as well.

Battery Maintenance

Some battery resellers offer special cell caps ("mushroom" battery caps) that actually condense and recycle the water that tries to escape the battery cells under a heavy charge. These special "caps" are well worth the extra money, since you will need to water the batteries less often and use far less distilled water. Distilled water is at a high premium at sea, as it is heavy and bulky. But batteries will not tolerate just any freshwater—you must use only steam-distilled or demineralized water. Steam-distilled water will test at approximately 0–5 parts per million (PPM) of dissolved solids.

As a comparison, the World Health Organization says that any water that has a salinity of less than 1,000 PPM is safe to drink and is considered freshwater. The water that comes from a desalination plant (water maker) working at peak performance is only 200–600 PPM) and therefore not suitable for use in batteries (except in an actual emergency). Likewise, the minerals in most tap, well, or spring water will also adversely affect the performance and longevity of any wet cell battery, and thus should never be used.

The bottom line is, you need to carry many gallons of distilled water on long voyages and check and top off your batteries on a regular schedule. The rate at which you'll need to add water to your batteries varies with how hard you are using them. I make it a point to check battery water levels every 90 days. There are some types of deep-cycle batteries that are sealed and are not serviceable (i.e., gel cell batteries). Make sure you understand which type you have.

Navigation Equipment

Before we get into high-tech gizmos, I want to stress that whatever equipment you buy, you still need to have all the old-school navigation basics as backup: paper charts of your entire area of operations, including the approaches, detailed charts of interesting islands and potential final destinations, pilot charts, nautical almanac, sextant, and the book *World Cruising Routes* (see Chapter 3).

Once you have chosen your ideal destination, make a trip to your local marine chandlery and have them put together a complete chart package covering the entire area of your route of travel, plus smaller-scale charts of individual landfalls, islands, and other interesting locations. If you are looking at an Atlantic Ocean destination, then I would buy the large-scale charts so that you have an overview of the entire ocean. The same goes for the Pacific.

One other general recommendation: For technical reasons it is important to use a dedicated battery bank for the navigation and communications systems. The details are beyond the scope of this book, but trust me: It's a good idea! The last thing you need is to have an emergency and need to use the radio, only to find that the batteries are dead because someone left too many toys or lights on somewhere.

Some folks posit that *everything* electrical will be toast should there be an HEMP attack, but that's not necessarily true.

If protected from an initial HEMP event, radar, autopilot, depth-finders, gyrocompasses, and flux-gate compasses will all be fully functional. There is now a considerable amount of equipment (EMP filters and shielding) that was formerly only available to the military that is now available for sale to the public. One online source for EMP filters for SSB and VHF radios is www.meteolabor .ch/en/emc-products/emp-protectors-csp-series. However, moving-map and chart-plotter machines may have intermittent usability issues if GPS satellites are knocked out, since they require at least three satellites to deliver a location fix of your position.

RADAR

Radar is critical for navigation at night or in fog and for surveillance at sea or at anchor. If you have two radar units onboard your boat, when you arrive at your island destination and set up a shore base, you can take one unit off the boat and install it onshore to monitor the waters around your island night and day. You will also need to move some solar panels and batteries and bring them ashore to power the radar—and any other equipment as desired. (For this reason it's important to have "more than enough" high-quality, deep-cycle batteries and solar panels installed on your boat, plus extra wiring, connectors, and such for the installation work.)

AUTOPILOT

Sometimes, an autopilot is the best crew onboard the boat. It steers a better course than any human can, doesn't need food or water, and never complains. Some commercial captains refer to their autopilot as "Iron Mike." Don't buy a cheap unit to save money, that's a huge mistake! In my opinion, Furuno U.S.A. makes the best units, period.

GPS

I hate to sound like a salesman for Furuno, but here again, Furuno is the absolute leader in commercial marine electronics (except for SSB radios, as discussed under "Communications Equipment"). A moving map GPS unit makes navigation as simple as it is in your car!

You will also need to buy electronic chart cards for your route and destination; these slide inside the GPS chart plotters. As with your paper charts, purchase every chart for your entire area of operations (Atlantic or Pacific), and get two of each card so you have a backup. I store all of these chart cards in special protective bags and then in metal tins to prevent damage from EMP or stray static discharges.

SONAR SYSTEM

A sonar system is important for finding depths, which can help verify your location on a chart as well as keep you from running aground. Here again, buy a Furuno unit.

OPTICS

All boats should have several sets of high-quality binoculars onboard. They are valuable for dead-reckoning navigation when you are within visual range of objects on land that can serve as landmarks. Binoculars are also important for situational awareness (knowing who's in your operating area), as well as surveillance and counter-surveillance.

Fujinon makes the best in my opinion, but I also own some Nikon and Leica optical equipment as well, and they have also proven to be first-rate.

Night-vision binoculars are a bit of a luxury, but I think they are well worth the financial sacrifice. On one ocean crossing, I could see the lights of the Hawaiian Islands from more than 200 miles away at night using night vision. Several companies make excellent quality products these days, so it pays to price shop and compare the actual performance of the optics.

Communications Equipment

The importance of communications equipment cannot be over stressed. It will allow you access information (that others may not be able to get) and find out what is going on. This can also provide a strategic advantage to you and your group.

If protected from an initial EMP or HEMP event, many ship's electronics, including communications gear, are still useful, as they function independently. For example:

Protected shortwave radios can function just fine post-HEMP/EMP and talk across thousands of miles to any other radio that was protected from the initial event. This includes weather fax machines, which work on the same frequencies as shortwave and SSB radios. On boats, the primary shortwave radio is the Marine Single Sideband Radio, or "SSB Radio" for short. These radios have high outputs, usually in excess of 100 watts of output power. Icom America has been making SSB radios for decades serving maritime, civilian, and military needs. Their marine-grade SSB radios are designed to be very robust and will withstand the long-term demands of a marine environment, where other radios may not. The frequencies used by these radios are able to bounce off the ionosphere, and because of that, these radios can reach and communicate with other SSB radios around the world, using a multitude of user-selected radio frequencies, each of which tends to work better at various distances and times of the day (most operator manuals discuss these dynamics). Amateur radio operators (ham radio) also use SSB radios on frequencies that are assigned to them by the FCC, and operators must have a ham license to operate on those assigned frequencies. The maritime frequencies that are assigned by FCC for vessels at sea require their own licensing. It should noted, however, that under FFC rules, in a genuine emergency, any operator may deviate from the rules and operate on an unassigned frequency as needed. Of course in the event of a total collapse of the national energy grid, I don't think the FCC is going to be too worried about the few remaining radio operators taking some liberties.

VHF radios are the same in most respects, except that their range is nominally under 50 miles. Normally, VHF radios are used in day-to-day operations between boats and their crews who are away from the boat.

All-in-all, if you have implemented some forms of HEMP countermeasures (EMP filters on radio wiring, etc.) and are using a steel boat, and maintain good situational awareness coupled with quick reaction to potential events, the odds of maintaining a nearly full complement of both navigation and communications equipment post-event are good.

SATELLITE TELEPHONE/EMAIL

In a regional disaster and some other events, satellite phones may still work when land lines and cell phones fail, for either voice communications or email. Iridium makes the best units and has the best service.

SATELLITE RADIO SYSTEM

Similarly, SiriusXM satellite radio might continue to provide news and information after some events even when land-based systems are down. A car system will work fine, so long as you make sure to buy the marine antenna and coaxial wiring for it.

SINGLE SIDEBAND/HAM RADIO

Single sideband (SSB) transceivers can transmit and receive calls around the world at some times of the day or night on certain frequencies. Under normal conditions, if properly installed, they can reliably communicate across 2,000 to 3,000 miles, sometimes across even greater distances.

Icom America makes the best radio gear in my opinion and given its robust construction and reliability represents a good investment in your security. The complete SSB radio installation requires the radio (in the neighborhood of $2,000), a tuner box (about $1,000 on its own), and an antenna (a long wire antenna is best; on a sailboat this is called a backstay antenna). With an add-on modem unit you can also use your SSB/ham radio to send and receive email over the transceiver. (However, the services of a ground station are needed to relay email between ships at sea and land-based computer networks.)

Note that if you are building a fiberglass or wooden vessel from scratch, you can have a ground-plane (counterpoise) for the SSB radio fiberglassed into the bottom of the hull, which will give a fiberglass vessel a more effective counterpoise nearly approximating that of a steel boat. Therefore, on some fiberglass hulls, a large copper screen of suitable dimensions can be integrated in between a final additional lamination inside the bilge of the hull. This screen is thereby fully encapsulated (which prevents corrosion) except for where it attaches to the grounding foil that runs to the shortwave radio chassis.

CITIZENS' BAND RADIO

Citizens' Band (CB) radio operates on frequencies different from SSB or VHF. These transceivers can work effectively across 20 miles or more at sea. Because they are relatively inexpensive, there are millions of them in public hands around the world. Having a CB radio provides one more way to reach out and find out what's going on. Cobra makes good base stations and handheld units.

VHF RADIO

Marine VHF radios can send and receive transmissions to a range of approximately 20 to 50 miles. This type of radio is handy for communicating ship to ship, ship to shore, and vice versa. In order to have this capability you'll need a base station aboard the boat and enough waterproof handheld units to equip your crew when they go ashore. Some people will simply use a handheld as the ship's main VHF radio. I strongly disagree with that. For one, a VHF base station unit has 20 watts of power output, so it can transmit much farther (the max distance) than a 5- or 6-watt handheld unit. Secondly, base stations have better receivers and bigger antennas so they can pick up faint signals much better than a handheld unit. Some VHF radios have built-in scramblers, which allow for totally private communications. Icom America makes the best units. The small handheld units also allow personnel onshore to communicate with each other.

WEATHER FAX

Weather fax units receive weather charts sent from land-based transmissions over shortwave radio frequencies using facsimile (fax) technology. It's possible that in a disaster these units could receive SITREPS (situation reports) and updates from land-based and sea-based stations. Furuno U.S.A. makes the best units.

WEATHER INSTRUMENTS

Other important basic weather prediction instruments to have onboard (and on land) are a barometer and devices to measure wind speed and direction, temperature, and humidity. The company Weems & Plath makes quality units, but many other manufacturers also sell high-quality units.

Environmental Equipment

This category of equipment is related to basic human health and comfort: clean water, sanitation, and climate control. The overall success or failure of long-term survival or voyaging is highly dependent upon morale, and morale is greatly affected by the environment. By maintaining an optimal environment for your crew, you help ensure your success.

POTABLE WATER

Most people can survive for weeks without food, but only a few days without water. On an expedition with four adults, a plan for strict water rationing would allow for a minimum of 2 gallons of freshwater per person per day for drinking and cooking: 8 gallons per day total. Using the sample plan from Chapter 1, the maximum 7,000-mile voyage would take 58 days, or 464 gallons of pure water—just for drinking and cooking.

You may be thinking, *But I can live on a gallon of water a day easily....* But remember, you won't be just lounging around in your air-conditioned home or car. Instead, you'll be working on deck and below on your watches in tropical and sub-tropical weather, and just doing basic chores will make you sweat much more than you think. In fact, some survival experts recommend anywhere from 12 to 30 liters of drinking water per day, per person, in arid and hot climates.

Still, I believe 2 gallons per person per day is a safe general minimum, but it doesn't cover additional water requirements needed in excessive heat, during hard labor, or both. In additional, you also want some freshwater for personal hygiene.

A 50-foot boat can easily accommodate a freshwater tank of 600 gallons, providing a whopping 136 gallons over our 464-gallon minimum requirement for luxuries— like a freshwater rinse after a seawater shower, or clean clothes. As this example illustrates, unless there is some way to augment the water in the tank, you will have to carefully monitor your freshwater use. I have a flow meter on our freshwater tank that shows exactly how much water we have pumped out of the tank and used (this is in addition to a tank gauge).

Fortunately, there are ways to augment your water supply: Rainwater can be collected with a simple tarp system and directed into the tank(s), and seawater can be turned into freshwater using a desalination plant (water maker). Of course, both of these options depend upon a certain amount of equipment and energy.

Water in the tank however is like money in a bank, and there's no overdraft protection. If you go dry, you have a very serious problem. For this reason, we have two pure water tanks on our boat. The larger of the two is 1,000 gallons. The second, located under the galley, contains 75 gallons of drinking water. We have a pressure water pump that sends water to the smaller tank from the main tank through a series of three special water filters (5 micron charcoal filter, 1 micron filter, and finally a 0.2 micron washable ceramic filter; similar to a Doulton filter). The smaller water tank under the galley is dedicated drinking water, and to avoid wasting any, that water can only be pumped out using a hand pump at the galley sink. For this purpose we use a bronze Fynspray brand hand-pump. And speaking of sinks, make sure the ones on your boat are deep. Shallow sinks have little utility and allow water to slop out in rough seas. Stainless steel bar sinks are small yet deep and are available at many home improvement stores.

Pressure Water Systems

All the other water fixtures on our boat are supplied by pressure water from the main tank and are equipped with flow restrictors.

If you are on a larger boat, say 35 to 50 feet or more, then you will probably need a pressure water system for sinks, showers, dishwasher, clothes washer, and so on. Most pumps are 12 volts and are reliable if installed properly. However, I've seen a demo unit being flaunted on YouTube by some "expert" preppers that was set up without any filter protection for the pump intake. They had a couple of downstream filters (Doulton, etc.) on the high-pressure side of the pump to clean the water, but that was it. This is an example of the blind teaching the blind. Anyone with real experience in these systems knows that you must have a stainless-steel mesh screen filter inline before the pump to protect the pump valves (or impellor) from becoming obstructed, causing the pump to fail. In hard-plumbed permanent systems, it's also important to have an accumulator tank in the water line on the pressure line from the pump. I have had excellent service from SUREflo pumps (www.shurflo.com). SUREflo also makes pumps designed for your seawater wash-down needs. Many boats will utilize seawater to augment the freshwater supply onboard. This can be done, for instance, by washing the deck off with seawater, doing the dishes with seawater and soap, and if freshwater stores permit, you can rinse with freshwater instead of seawater. The same goes for personal hygiene and bathing; you can shower or bathe with seawater and take a quick rinse with freshwater. Ladies with long hair will especially appreciate rinsing their hair with freshwater (goes to morale). So as you see, having a pressurized seawater supply system can also serve many purposes.

Desalination Plant

I like to plan on having both rain-catch and desalination options available on an expedition cruise. Under most conditions offshore, these two methods of augmenting water supplies onboard will provide ample freshwater on a very long-term basis—even years.

Many desalination systems, or water makers, are commercially available today. Some work better than others, and some are more reliable than others, regardless of what manufacturers and salesmen say. This is mission-critical equipment. Don't buy a cheap unit to save money! I have used several manufacturers' water makers over the years. My recommendation is Village Marine Tec (a division of Parker Racor) for desalination plants; they make the best units, in my opinion. The unit that we are using on our current ship has approximately 5,840 hours of use on the same system (high-pressure membranes, pump, etc.) over a four-year period, and the unit is still going strong six years later. During the four years of the expedition, I replaced the pre-filters (like under-sink water filters) several times, and the brushes in the 12-volt motor twice. (All of this maintenance can be done with very basic tools and know-how.)

In that time, our water maker has delivered over 60,000 gallons of freshwater! That allowed us to use about 41 gallons of pure freshwater per day—allowing everyone onboard to have a couple of showers every day and all the water we can drink, plus rinsing off our diving gear and the boat deck.

That said, using water properly takes practice! I like to start training the crew by having them take all their showers using a "solar shower" unit—basically a one-gallon plastic bag connected to a hose and shower head. By using this limited amount of water to shower every day for a week or two, you quickly learn how to take a one-gallon shower and get it done. After that, you can come pretty close to the same usage in the indoor shower.

Rainwater Catchment System

Catching rainwater can significantly augment your water supply, especially in the equatorial tropics where there are frequent rain squalls. A large polypropylene tarp can be fitted to a 1-inch diameter hose. If you've kept the tarp clean, you can tie it up to the standing rigging (or between palm trees if you are on land) when you determine that rain is coming and direct the hose into the fill spout for the water tank. If you happen to be on land, you will have to improvise some form of storage. If the tarp hasn't been kept clean, then once it starts raining you vent the water into a bucket (for laundry use later) until the tarp has been rinsed clean, and then direct the water hose from the trap into the ship's water tank.

SANITATION SYSTEM (SEWAGE)

The U.S. Coast Guard (USCG) has guidelines for the discharge of materials from vessels at sea. Check with those guidelines and then draw up a management plan for your boat. We treat all black water (sewage) with a USCG Type II treatment plant and then store that sewage in a holding tank when we are moored or operating at inshore waters. At sea (outside 20 miles), we use the same plant to treat all sewage before discharge pursuant to USCG regulations. These practices would be important to observe at any small tropical island where you would set up in a lagoon to live for a year or longer.

AWNINGS

Good awnings are critical in sunny areas. Since they provide shade, they're an important commodity in tropical lower latitudes. On sailboats, most people will hang them over the mainsail or mizzen-mast booms to form a tent-like cover, tying the sides to the port and starboard safety railings. I prefer the awnings sold in garden-supply stores for covering outdoor growing areas. They are made of a woven polyethylene and allow air to pass through while stopping 90 percent of the UV rays. These garden awnings come in various colors, including blue, green, and black.

The other popular awning material is called Sunbrella. It is more expensive and doesn't allow air to pass through, although unlike the woven poly, it will keep rain off. In the tropics, however, I have found that the 70° to 80° rainwater isn't a problem for most crew. But our boat also has hard cover over the back deck if anyone wants to stay out of the rain.

HEATING AND AIR CONDITIONING

If you're bugging out to colder locations, heating could be a mandatory piece of equipment. There are several brands of quality diesel stoves and heaters that will heat a boat very well. Some larger boats in Alaska use wood stoves or pellet stoves to heat the living spaces. Propane is the last choice in my book because it can explode; propane is heavier than air, and leaked gas will accumulate in the lowest part of the boat and silently wait under there until it is ignited by any electrical spark. Propane is also harder to obtain in some places, more so than wood or diesel.

In a tropical climate, air conditioning might be something to consider, although it is definitely not a necessity. This will be the first to be crossed off your wish list if the budget or space onboard is lacking.

Modern Conveniences

INSIDE ELECTRIC LIGHTING

Inside lights aren't as critical as outside lights. Though halogen is brighter than LEDs, it may not be worth the expense of power used indoors. So if you can afford the cost of LED fixtures, this is a good way to save electrical power.

WATER HEATER

Good water heaters use the hot water from the engine's cooling system via thermal transfer across a metal barrier to heat the water in the tank. Electricity can also be used to augment this system. All-electric water heating is another option, but not the best. Make sure the water heater tank is stainless steel so it doesn't rust out.

CABIN FANS

Cabin fans are important for personal cooling in warm seasons and in tropical areas. They are most efficient if they point directly at the sleeping area (bunk), since it's important to be able to sleep comfortably below deck on the ship. Otherwise, you may be sleeping on deck.

REFRIGERATOR AND FREEZER

On our boat, we use two GE Energy Star top-load freezer units purchased at Home Depot—one as a refrigerator. I converted it by switching out the freezer thermostat with a refrigerator thermostat that I bought at Grainger Supply. It's been running 24/7 for the past six years without a glitch, and this is the second time I have made this adaptation with great success.

Top loaders are essential for saving thermal energy on boats or wherever power is in short supply. Cold air acts like water and spills out the front door of standing units whenever the door is opened, forcing the unit to re-cool the entire air mass inside each time the door is opened. Top loaders are like swimming pools: The cold air stays in place. Plus, the contents are less likely to shift (disastrously) with the motion of the boat.

DISHWASHER

Most dishwashers clean dishes better than any human and use less water. There are countertop dishwashers available that I believe use as little as 1.5 gallons per load. On our current vessel we have a stainless steel Whirlpool dishwasher, which has served well over the last six years.

LAUNDRY MACHINE

We find that clean clothes are important for morale and health. On our current boat we have a Whirlpool stacked washer-dryer unit that is awesome. Designed to fit in a closet space, this model comes in both 120 VAC and 240 VAC-powered units (the latter dries more quickly). In my opinion, these separate units work better than some of the all-in-one washer-dryers (especially when it comes to drying clothes quickly), such as those made by Splendide and some other companies. For one, the all-in-one units tend to use 120 VAC and the dryer heating element isn't as effective as the 220 VAC heating elements available in the standalone dryers. Also, if you're already running your generator (fuel use is limited), you'll want to be doing both washing and drying concurrently (if you have several loads). However, if available space is an issue, then a compromise may be reasonable. Otherwise, stick with Whirlpool or Maytag stacked or singles if you have the space. Beyond these modern solutions, there's the time-honored washboard and clothes line—we have those, too.

MICROWAVE CONVECTION OVEN

A microwave convection oven is a great appliance for cooking since they use so little power. Also, there is no fire or smoke. And popcorn goes a long way for snacks!

WASTE MANAGEMENT SYSTEMS

For food scraps, a garbage disposal is another useful galley appliance. Be sure to buy a stainless steel unit only.

The U.S. Coast Guard has guidelines about the discharge of all materials from vessels at sea. Check with those guidelines and then draw up a management plan for your boat. We use a combination of methods that includes disposing of allowable materials at sea and storing some other materials after compacting, later discharging those compacted materials into an approved landfill or burning them in a permitted area. If you happen to be using a wood stove for heating your boat, then you can burn some of the garbage that doesn't emit any foul odors and get some fuel in the process.

ENTERTAINMENT SYSTEMS

We find that audio and video entertainment are important for maintaining morale. In addition to a couple of Sony car CD decks with amplifiers and quality speakers, we also have several iPods with headphones.

Similarly, we have two video systems: one in the main living area and one in the captain's cabin. We have a movie night onboard at least once a week where the crew all gets together with popcorn and other goodies. Everyone has a good time.

Maintenance and Repairs

You cannot imagine the importance of having an extensive selection of hand and power tools onboard a vessel that is heading to any remote location. I could fill chapters with the stories of other sailors who've had an equipment failure in a remote location and were having to tough it out until I happened by and fixed what was broken, in some cases, only because I had the tools to get the job done.

It can be something as important as a generator or a main engine or something as simple as a personal music player, as was the case with the captain of a National Geographic research ship *Sea Bird*, whose only source of music on a long-range voyage was his Sony Discman. When I saw this very large ship pulling into a cove off an island where we were anchored, we gave them a call on the VHF to see what they were up to. After chatting with the captain for a bit, I learned that he was bummed out because his disc player was broken and he had no tunes to help pass the day. Being set up to install and repair electronics, I told him I might be able to fix his Discman, so he sent a crewman over with it. Using a magnifying visor and my jeweler's toolkit I opened it up and discovered that a tiny rubber drive belt had fallen off a pulley. I put the belt back in place, cleaned some parts, closed the unit, inserted a CD, and it worked great. I sent it back to the captain and then continued with my own day, cleaning oysters for dinner.

About an hour later, my son yelled, "Hey Dad, that big Zodiac is headed back over here!" The Zodiac pulled alongside our boat and the crew members started tossing cases of steaks, other food, and beer up onto our deck, exclaiming, "Our captain says thanks!" My son and I looked on in wonder, both of us grinning ear to ear. It was clear that I had made the ship's captain a happy man, and my reward paid for the tools I had used many times over, as well as for the short time I spent on that small project.

For a prepper who has suddenly shifted into full survival mode, having a skill that is in high demand and can be bartered could be an invaluable asset. Most of the time, when other sailors want to hire me to make repairs to engines or electronics, I simply take cash for my efforts. However, after a worldwide apocalypse, cash won't be worth the paper it's printed on, and as my dad used to say, it doesn't even make for good toilet paper. Gold, silver, and other such commodities are also useless for barter in such a scenario. The things that are worth something are food, pure water, clothing and footwear, medicine, cigarettes, alcohol, fuel, weapons, fishing equipment, ammunition, equipment, parts for key equipment, and the skills to fix things when they break! On most islands, fishing hooks and monofilament fishing line are in high demand and can be easily traded for food (fish, bananas, coconuts), water, or other commodities.

Doctors, dentists, mechanics, electricians, welders, plumbers, blacksmiths, farmers, and some others will all be able to barter services for goods they need.

Having a complete, professional set of tools, and knowing how to use them, assures that you can fix your own stuff and gives you the option to barter your services for things you might need.

A good selection of tools is worth more than gold, but only a little less heavy! Plan on having a hundred pounds of tools onboard. (Here's another way that having a bigger boat pays off!)

HAND TOOLS

When you acquire tools, buy the best quality you can afford. To save money, look for quality tools at garage sales. Husky, Craftsman (Sears), Proto, and Snap-on brand tools have lifetime warranties and are solid professional-quality hand tools. Again, you cannot have too many tools on a boat, because even taking great care, it's amazing how many will end up in the drink!

Socket Sets

I recommend buying a full set of ¼-inch sockets, including deep and short sockets, a ⅜-inch drive socket set with both short and deep sockets, and a full ½-inch socket set with short and deep sockets. Normally if you go up to 1⅜-inch-size sockets on the ½-inch set, you'll have sockets large enough to handle most jobs on most diesel engines and transmissions. You should also match that same general range of sizes in metric sockets—both deep and short.

Wrenches, Pliers, and Cutters

You'll also want to have a full metric and U.S. set of Allen drivers to match your ⅜- or ½-inch socket driver. I would also recommend buying both ⅜-inch and ½-inch torque wrenches. A full set of driver extensions, swivels, and adapters are also a must.

The same goes for end wrenches; buy them up to 1⅜-inch size, and get two or three of the common size wrenches: ⅜, ⁷⁄₁₆, ½, ⁹⁄₁₆, ⅝, ¹¹⁄₁₆, ¾, and ⅞. Full sets of ratcheting end wrenches, in both U.S. and metric sizes, are great to have as well.

I also carry a set of four crescent wrenches that ranges from a small to a very large wrench that can handle nuts and bolts up to 2 inches.

You can't go wrong having a full set of genuine channel lock pliers, including the really big ones. A set of three sizes of pipe wrenches is also important, including a large one. A strap wrench is an important tool for removing canister filters. And several sizes of bolt cutters will come in handy. You should have a few sets of vise grip pliers, slip joint pliers, diagonal cutting pliers, and wire strippers.

Screwdrivers

You should have full U.S. and metric sets of Phillips- and straight-blade screwdrivers, as well as a full set of Torx drivers and Allen wrenches. Go up to ¾-inch in U.S. sizes and up to 18 mm in metric. A good set of jeweler's screwdrivers, tweezers, cutters, and pliers is also important to have for fine work.

Hammers

A good selection of hammers is important to have: small and large ball-peen hammers, small and large dead-blow hammers, one claw hammer, and small and large sledge hammers, say 2-pound and 5-pound.

Chisels, Punches, and Drifts

A really good set of hard cold chisels, punches, and drifts is important to have in all sizes. You should also have a couple of different sizes of tapered punches and soft bronze drifts to drive steel pins with.

Files

A full set of files is also important to have, ranging from very small flat, round, rat-tail, and triangular files to the same shapes in larger sizes, including a large mill bastard file.

Calipers and Gauges

Tools for measuring metal parts are important to have, such as a metal dial caliper, Vernier calipers, metal ruler, awl, steel dividers, inside and outside calipers, depth gauge, drill gauge, and two sets of steel feeler gauges (U.S. and metric).

Drill Bits

A superset of cobalt drill bits is the minimum. (I carry three sets that range from $\frac{1}{32}$ inch up to 1 inch). You also need full tap-and-die sets in both U.S. and metric sizes, with extra taps in the common smaller sizes up to $\frac{1}{2}$ inch, since they are very brittle and can snap off very easily. I also recommend a full set of extractors (easy outs).

Plumbing and Electrical Tools

You should have a full kit for working with copper tubing and steel pipes, including common pipe taps and dies up to ¾-inch NPT size and a reamer. For copper tubing you'll need Rigid brand steel tube cutters in large and small sizes with extra blades, a flaring tool, and a reamer.

A MAPP gas brazing torch with solder and flux is also a necessity for some repairs, such as soldering heavy-gauge wires (battery cables) or repairing sheet metal. Additionally, large and small (for circuit board repairs) soldering irons and a couple spools of different gauges of flux-core solder are important for electrical repairs. I also carry a Weller soldering gun, which heats up very fast and is good for faster repairs on most size wires.

Other Small Tools

You should also include the following in your toolkit:
- Hand hacksaw with cobalt blades and keyhole saws
- Small hand drill (the kind you actually crank by hand!)

POWER TOOLS

I like the DeWalt brand of rechargeable, battery-operated power tools and recommend having a full set, including a drill-motor with ⅜-inch chuck, belt sander, 90-degree angle drill (⅜-inch chuck), and router.

You should also have the following:
- An excellent set of saws, including battery-powered and 120 VAC Sawzalls (made by Milwaukee), along with a very large and redundant

assortment of bimetal (cobalt-steel) blades to handle wood and metal, a circular saw, and a jigsaw.

- Both battery-operated and AC-powered drill motors with ⅜-inch chucks.
- 4½-inch angle grinder and a selection of grinding and cutoff discs and wire wheels for that unit.
- Air-powered ½-inch drive impact wrench.
- Air-powered die grinder with a large assortment of bits and grinding wheels in all shapes.
- Pneumatic drill with ⅜-inch chuck.
- Professional Dremel tool with large assortment of bits, wheels, and saw blades.
- Air hammer with a set of bits, drivers, and chisels.

WELDING EQUIPMENT

If you have a steel boat, it makes good sense to have at least one welder onboard. Even if you don't have a steel boat, there are a lot of steel parts that can break, and when there are no repair shops, where can you go to get a welding job done? So it's better to have a welder (and know how to use it)! Since I do a lot of metalworking for others and myself on occasion, we have three welders on our current vessel: a cutting/brazing torch (oxygen-acetylene rig), a MIG welder, and an arc welder (buzz box or stick welder). For small jobs where you need a heat range close to oxy-acetylene, an MAPP gas torch is very handy; it burns much hotter than a propane torch.

A 200/225-amp AC arc welder with assorted stainless steel and mild steel welding rods is the minimum. If you are on a larger steel boat, I also recommend a second wire-feed welder (MIG welder) with assorted stainless and mild steel wire spools.

For the MIG welder, you'll need to carry both CO_2 gas for steel and tri-mix gas for stainless steel work, along with a regulator. These gases can be purchased in smaller pony bottles, which are very easy to move around and store.

With either setup you will need the basic welding necessities, including a leather apron and welding gloves, a helmet with at least a 10 shade (some people prefer darker shades), slag/chipping hammer, wire brush, and some vise grips that will take a beating.

Either of these welding machines requires a generator with a continuous output of at least 4.5 kW (kilowatt) for average welding jobs using less than half of the rated welder output (up to 80 amps welding output). On the 225-amp AC arc welder I have run $\frac{1}{16}$, $\frac{1}{8}$, and $\frac{3}{32}$ 6011/6013 and 308L/309L welding rod at ranges from 40 to 80 amps using my smaller diesel generator (4.5 KW).

Many commercially made welders operate at 40 volts direct current, so if you find yourself in a pinch without any generator to power your welder, you can make a DC welder by wiring three 12-volt batteries in series to make a 36-volt power supply. This welder will run welding rod from $\frac{1}{8}$ to $\frac{3}{32}$ of an inch.

It's not even that complicated. To connect the three batteries in series you start by connecting a short heavy-gauge (#2 or larger) wire from the positive terminal on the first battery to the negative terminal on the second battery.

Then you connect another short, heavy-gauge wire from the positive terminal on the second battery to the negative terminal on the third battery. Now the three batteries are connected in series.

The only terminals without any connections are the positive terminal on the third battery and the negative terminal on the first battery. You then connect a welding cable (or one half of a set of car jumper cables) to the empty positive terminal on the third battery and clamp the other end of that cable to the work (whatever it is you are intending to weld). Then you connect another welding cable (or the other half of the car jumper cable) to the empty negative terminal on the first battery, and the other end of that cable to the welding rod. Now your 36-volt DC welder is almost ready to use.

Once you have double checked that all of your wiring is properly connected, you'll need to cover the batteries with a leather cover, or something else that sparks from arc welding cannot burn or penetrate, because when you are welding you will be discharging the batteries and they will be producing hydrogen gas, which is highly explosive.

I also recommend doing the welding as far away from the batteries as your cables will allow. It's prudent to keep a fire extinguisher close by during any welding operations, as well as a bucket of water and wet rag to cool things off as needed.

You need to pay close attention to the batteries so as not to overheat them. Remember, you will be drawing a lot of current when you're welding, and the batteries will heat up. The time it takes them to heat up will depend on the size and capacity of the batteries that are used, so it's wise to make a short weld and then stop and check the batteries for any signs of overheating. If they get hot (more than 120°F), just stop welding and wait until they cool down before proceeding, taking intermittent breaks as needed until you have completed the weld. When you are done, carefully disconnect all the cables from all the batteries. Then check the water in the battery cells and add distilled water as needed before recharging the batteries.

HOOKAH DIVING SYSTEM

This diving equipment is important to have on a boat for a few reasons. First, it allows you to work under the boat for extended periods. You can stay down an unlimited time at the depth of most ships (less than 30 feet), so a hookah rig avoids the need to fill scuba tanks and crawl on and off deck during a repair. Second, it also allows you to dive for the mollusks that are a bit too deep for snorkeling gear without a scuba tank. We have two hookah lines: a 150-foot line for hull cleaning and maintenance, and a 300-foot line for deep salvage work and spear fishing (see "Fishing Gear," below).

AIR COMPRESSORS

Two types of air compressor are useful. A low-pressure compressor (120 PSI) is needed for air tools and hookah diving. DeVilbiss makes good compact units that will serve well. If you intend to also use it for hookah diving, then you need to install an inline series of Norgren air filters to remove all water, oil vapor, and impurities from the compressor air, making it "certified breathable air."

A high-pressure air compressor (3,000–4,000 PSI) is needed for filling scuba tanks. Bauer makes the best units. They can be powered by either a Honda gas engine or 120 VAC electric motor, depending on your needs. Basic units cost around $6,000.00 new. By having a 120 VAC-powered compact air compressor, that uses a small ½ horsepower AC electric motor, it can be powered with a 2,000-watt inverter, which uses 12 VDC from the battery banks (remember there is a 2,000-watt surge power requirement on the inverter during the AC motor startup). This combination provides a power source option in the event the AC generator is out of operation and allows you another way to use your Hookah dive system. I like and recommend a DeVilbiss or equivalent brand compressor, with an air dryer installed between the compressor and any air tools, and at least 50 feet of air-hose and fittings.

FIXED TOOLS

The following large, fixed tools are important (or at least nice) to have:

- A two-wheel bench grinder (fine and course wheels).
- A small drill press with ½-inch chuck. Some jobs are simply best done with a drill press. If you have a place for one, you'll find it a good investment in money and space.
- An arbor press is great for working on parts that have pressed shafts. It doesn't need much room.

- Life without a good bench vise is miserable—don't leave home without one! A large bench vise with an anvil is essential. I also have a smaller one that can clamp onto any tabletop that's great for working on small projects, electronics, and the like.
- A lathe. Our current boat doesn't have one onboard, but I would like to have a lathe with a 6-foot bed. It takes a lot of room but is the centerpiece of any machine shop for good reason.

SPARE PARTS

Once you have installed or arrived at all the equipment that will be onboard your boat, you will need to carefully go through each of the operations and repair manuals and make a catalog list of all the parts that will require scheduled replacements: oil filters, fan belts, rubber impellors (I recommend nitrile rubber impellors over BUNA rubber impellors), starters, alternators, fuel injectors, gaskets, O rings, special batteries, fuses, light bulbs, fluids, and stainless steel hardware, including threaded screws, bolts, nuts, sheet metal and wood screws, and so on.

This process must be done with very careful consideration to the kinds of parts failures that will certainly occur over time. It's easy to forecast the need for oil and filters and the like, but things like fuel injectors for a diesel engine are not as obvious. It's best to work with an experienced consultant (not a salesman) in this regard. You needn't face a steep learning curve if you have a good consultant who can get you squared away and help you learn in the process.

Fishing Gear

Sailors often neglect to equip a boat with proper fishing gear. In survival situations, that omission could have adverse affects, causing you to use up your stored goods at a much faster rate. The following details the minimum complement of gear I would advise for any boat.

First of all, the boat needs to be set up with at least four really sturdy rod holders at the stern so that when you are under way you can troll as many fishing rods with jigs as possible. Don't settle for just one or two holders as some people do—that's a mistake. Tuna travel in schools, and when they come up to the surface to feed, they will bite every jig they see. It's easy to hook four fish at once, but only if you have four lines with jigs out. By the time you reel in the fish and start again, the odds of getting into the school again are low, which is why you want to catch as many as possible at the first opportunity. In order to troll four lines at the same time, they must be spread apart and staggered in length behind the boat so that they do not get tangled. This requires just a bit of practice, but essentially, it works like this: You will have one line that is what we'll call the "long" line, which you put out before any other line, and of course when you retrieve the lines, it's the last one you will reel into the boat. The rod holders for the two longest lines should be mounted opposite each other on the port and starboard rails about 5 to 10 feet forward of the stern rail. Of these two lines, the longest line and jig should trail behind the boat about 100 feet, or two to three boat lengths. The next longest line and jig will be dropped back about 75 feet, and is run from the opposite side of the boat. Then we have what we'll call the two "short" lines, which are operated from the stern railing, with rod holders positioned at each of the stern quarters. So this means that these two rod holders are mounted on the stern railing with as much separation as possible. Of the two short lines, one will be run out longer than the other. So the longer of the two short lines will be operated from the stern railing on same side of the boat as the longest of the long lines. This line will be run out behind the boat about 50 feet. And finally, on the opposite side of stern rail will be the shortest line, which is run out about 25 feet.

One important technique is to slow the boat down when you hookup, but never stop the boat; otherwise fish that are hooked will swim past and under the boat, which is a bad thing. Before angling any fish, quickly reel in any lines that have no fish. You can slow the boat's speed to make angling easier, but never allow the boat to come to a stop; always keep it moving slow-ahead (usually engine idling speed). Always angle the fish that is closest to the boat first, especially when you have multiple fish on at the same time. This clears the shortest lines out of the way before you angle fish on the longer lines.

Once you angle the fish to a position alongside the boat, you can either use a net or a hook-gaff to bring the fish onto the deck of the boat. One way people lose fish is by trying to net a fish improperly. Never put the net behind the fish (netting it tail-first). Always net the fish head-first, because the fish will help the process by swimming into the net.

Once you have a tuna, or any other large fish on deck, you subdue the fish with a club (I use a small aluminum bat) and then insert a sharp filet knife into the fish's head just behind the back edge of the gill plate and push the knife through the fish. This will sever the artery that is located between the heart and gills, and the fish will bleed out very quickly, which is ideal. Dorado (or mahi mahi) also travel in schools, just like tuna; therefore, you can catch several fish at once if you are properly prepared by having as many lines rigged and in the water as possible anytime you are under way in areas that are suitable for such fishing.

On our boats we install six rod holders spaced apart on the stern and side rails. Sometimes, we get six fish at the same time, and then it's easy to fill the freezer fast. And once the freezer is full of filets, you can start drying fish for storage as well. Of course, it's not a bad idea to eat fresh sashimi and grilled tuna as well.

Each person onboard should be provided with at least two fishing rods: one lightweight rod for inshore fishing (IGFA 12-pound-class rod and reel) and one deep sea rod and reel (IGFA 50-pound-class rod and reel). I like using synthetic braided line on my deep sea setup, which is very thin yet extremely strong. As an example, the 50-pound test braid has the same diameter as 8-pound-test monofilament line. By using the stronger, thinner line, you will lose less gear over the long run both because it's less likely to break and because more line will fit on the reel compared to monofilament line of comparable strength. This is a great added feature when you hook into a really big fish, as it's harder for it to take all your line. On the 50-pound-class reel, you can use 80-pound-test synthetic braid.

In addition to these rods and reels, it's good to have a few spinning rods and reels for casting from shore or the boat. Here again, a stout rod and reel will pay off. Don't buy cheap fishing rods and reels; they don't hold up over the long term. Stick with Penn or Shimano reels and quality rods. It's also important to have the lubricant to service the reels periodically. Stock one spare fishing rod (no reel) for each weight class, as well. Rods are easily broken or damaged in many ways, and can be difficult to successfully repair, depending on where the damage is located.

Make sure you buy plenty of spare line for the reels, as well as a big commercial spool of 50-pound-test monofilament line (5,000 yards) as backup. In many places in the Caribbean, Mexico, South America, and the equatorial and South Pacific islands, the fishermen use hand lines to fish from shore and boats. Often these hand lines are made up with 50-pound monofilament line, so it's good barter material. It can also be used on your own reels if you have the need.

I also carry many spools of monofilament fluorocarbon leader material in 20-, 30-, 50-, and 80-pound test. Fish cannot see fluorocarbon line (I use Seaguar brand), unlike other types of clear monofilament. Normally, you would have a snap swivel tied to the main line coming from the reel, and the jig or the baited hook is made onto a 3- to 5-foot length of leader material (depending on the type of fishing), which is connected to a ball-bearing snap swivel.

The reason for the leader is twofold: First, the leader is usually lighter weight and harder for the fish to see. Second, if the line gets hooked on the bottom, or if a monster fish grabs on, you don't break off into the main line.

Lures and jigs come in almost every color and shape, so stick with the basics, but have dozens in various types. Most fishing tackle shops have good selections of salt- and freshwater jigs. For tuna and dorado, one of the most productive jigs is what is known as a cedar plug, which looks like a short piece of tapered wooden dowel with a lead tip and a big hook. Some of them are painted, and all seem to work well. I use all the colors and the plain wooden ones as well. Dorado like to bite jigs that are green and yellow.

There are also plastic jigs made by Zuker's, which come in a host of colors and sizes. I have great success with jigs that are 4 to 6 inches long, in white, blue, red, pink, yellow, green, and blends of those same colors. Some have silver metal flake in them, and they also work well.

It's important to have a large assortment of stainless steel hooks made by Mustad. You'll need single hooks ranging from #3 all the way up to #8 in size. I also carry a large assortment of stainless steel double hooks in the same sizes for use on my tuna jigs. Generally speaking, the bigger the hook, the stronger the leader will need to be. And you don't want a hook so large that the plastic skirt on the jig doesn't cover (hide) the hook by at least 70 to 90 percent. In other words, it's OK if the hook shows a bit, but not too much.

Sometimes you need to use live bait, which can be caught in one of two ways: using small shrimp fly jigs or with a cast net. Shrimp fly jigs come already tied up and ready to use. You simply add a suitable lead weight to one end of the line of flies and attach the other end to your snap swivel off the main line from the reel. The package has easy-to-follow instructions for making these connections. Then you lower the line over the side and start jigging at different depths until you find some fish. Usually, you'll catch several at the same time since there are about seven hooks on the rig. When you bring the bait fish aboard, you'll want to have a large container full of seawater ready to receive the fish so they stay alive. The other alternative is a live bait well, which seawater is continuously pumped into through a small plastic tank on deck, sort of like an aquarium. Sometimes I catch bait at night under the boat's stern lights shining in the water and then use that live bait the next morning to catch large yellowtail and grouper.

Another way to catch live bait is to use a cast net. It takes a bit of practice to learn to effectively cast the net— usually a day or two will suffice to master the moves. Once you've done that, it's easy to catch 20 to 50 small bait fish with each cast of the net. The person throwing the net usually stands knee to waist deep in the water.

Once the bait fish are caught they are stored in a large bucket of seawater that must be freshened (oxygenated) every so often until they can be transferred into a live bait well. In a pinch, if you're hungry, the 4- to 8-inch fish you catch in a throw net can be cooked, or depending on the species, may be tasty eaten raw with a bit of horseradish.

I also recommend carrying a couple of spear guns (see "Weapons Onboard" in Chapter 5), a couple of Hawaiian sling spears, snorkeling gear (mask, fins, snorkel, and dive knife), a lightweight neoprene wetsuit along with booties and a hood, and a mesh net "goody bag." With these items you can collect fish, lobsters, clams, oysters, and mussels in amazing quantities.

Provisioning

Most preppers will already have a good understanding of the math related to the daily calories needed to live. Our example scenario of provisioning for four adults for six months is ample to cover many contingencies, including a lengthy stopover before reaching our most distant possible destination in New Zealand. Any meal plan must be built around providing at least 2,500 calories per person per day, which takes into consideration calories needed for an active lifestyle. If we do the math for our six-month of stores for four adults, then we are looking at a total of 10,000 calories per day, multiplied by 180 days, or 1,800,000 total calories in meals stored aboard the boat. These provisions would be augmented to some degree or another by fishing and possibly hunting. We have found that through the effective use of our fishing skills, our stored provisions lasted three times as long as planned. In fact, on our latest four-year expedition, when we returned to our home port in the U.S. we still had enough stored provisions for another year. We could have genuinely lived off the sea, although some people will grow tired of eating seafood twice a day every day.

VARIETY AND MORALE

With that consideration in mind, if you're smart, most of the food you bring will be largely dependent on what you and your crew *like* eating. I love eating fresh-caught tuna and dorado and can eat it daily, and quite happily so. But not everyone enjoys seafood as much as I do; it never ceases to amaze me that some crewmembers will grow tired of eating these delicacies, including lobster, after only a few weeks. But some do.

Morale can fail if the complaints about not having anything "good to eat" become a daily occurrence. So my advice is to lay in plenty of the good old standbys, such as pasta (for some unknown reason, kids love Kraft macaroni and cheese), chili (with meat and beans), Spam (some people love this fried) and other canned meats, dehydrated mashed potatoes, and the like. I like to talk about food with my crew before we leave port and discover their favorite foods so we can provision those items in adequate quantities, and it should be no different for survival purposes.

Personally, I take exception to the idea that survival mode means surviving on freeze-dried meals and MREs. I believe you can eat the foods you normally enjoy, as long as those foods are part of the provisioning plan. Nothing could be worse for morale than to be thrust into the survival mode and forced to rely on provisions that taste like flavored sawdust. If you think I'm wrong, buy some freeze-dried stuff and MREs, and try feeding just that to your family for a week straight. See how that goes before you lay in stores of these items. If the complaints mount under ideal conditions, imagine how much worse it will be under duress.

There's nothing wrong with MREs; I just like the way other foods taste a lot more, and my crewmembers agree. These days, we have many options for long-lasting foods. One of a myriad of examples are the shitake mushrooms we found at Costco for a reasonable price. Besides the fact that they are a highly proven medicinal mushroom by naturopathic doctors, they taste great! The ones we bought were dehydrated and well sealed in large, heavy plastic bags. So as part of our provisioning for our last multiyear voyage, we bought a couple of dozen bags and stored them in the bilge with all the other overstock of supplies. Four years later, we still have a few bags of those mushrooms—and they still taste great!

Hopefully, your provisions will also be significantly augmented by fishing—an important skill for all mariners and survivalists. And once onshore at almost any island destination, where food sources are plentiful, in addition to fishing, you will be collecting mollusks, crabs, lobsters, seaweed, coconuts, and other terrestrial vegetation, thereby adding variety and calories to your stores of provisions.

In some areas, there may also be game animals to be had. Islanders have told me that you can learn to prepare a rat so that it actually tastes good. If this is true, there would be plenty of food on many islands from the ample rat populations. Seabirds are edible, in a pinch, but I am told they taste very gamey and fishy. Nonetheless, with a pellet rifle, it would be easy to hunt and kill as many birds and rats as necessary to survive in absence of any provisions in most locations.

PROVISIONING AND STORAGE

Some aspects of provisioning, like fishing and hunting for food, are dependent on destination and area of operations and having certain pieces of equipment onboard, including refrigeration. Some of your provisions may be in the form of frozen and refrigerated foods, and certain medicines also require the use of a freezer or refrigerator. These cooling units employ small compressors (as well as water pumps in some keel-cooled models) and therefore require a constant source of electricity. This means, as previously discussed, careful design and planning of the ship's electrical systems (charging and storage) are quite important considerations.

Another important consideration is that the foods brought aboard must store well for a long time in a humid environment. You need to use vacuum-packing equipment and airtight containers, such as resealable food grade 5-gallon plastic buckets. Glass jars can also be used for food storage if care is taken.

Canned foods are fine, so long as they are protected from humidity (rust). We store all of our canned goods inside vinyl tubs with lids so that they stay stacked and dry. The vinyl tubs sit on top of the rubber mats in storage areas (see Chapter 3). Similarly, we don't keep any goods in their original cardboard boxes onboard the boat. The hollow spaces in corrugated cardboard can harbor all kinds of small insects and their eggs, which can hatch once you're at sea. Also, paper packaging provides no protection from humidity.

I like to have a wide variety of stored goods, such as things like well-packaged, ready-to-eat snacks that contain a good source of protein and calories; Clif Bars are a good example (250 calories, 11 grams of protein). I also like to provision with old-old-school things like dried beans and other legumes, rice, oats, wheat flour, and other raw whole grains, which can be made into flour as needed using a hand-cranked grain mill. And of course you would want a considerable selection of canned goods—standard prepper fare (like canned chili and beans). On a boat, the key is to have lots of long-lasting, ready-to-eat goodies for times when you cannot prepare food, along with foods that require some preparation.

In my opinion, supplies don't need to last more than five years, and we always buy items that have a use-by date that provides five or more years of shelf life. When we are in port, we use the older supplies/foods first and then add the newer replacements behind or under the older goods, so they are consumed in the proper order. We also never let the basic stores become depleted from use. This way, we are always ready to go, and we always have a great selection of tasty supplies. So if some disaster were to occur, and we departed in a hurry for the open sea, all of our stored supplies would last at least two to three years or more, which is more than enough.

CHAPTER 5
Boat Security

Some people harbor unrealistic fears about having their boat taken during a crises, and that is a great place to start this chapter.

Before we start discussing security and security equipment, let's compare land-based security measures, such as bunkers and similar concepts, to the nautical prepping paradigm. This is a fair comparison when you consider that the cost of a fully stocked bunker is equal to or more than the cost of buying and stocking a used sailboat in the 40-foot class.

From my chair, most underground bunkers present a very risky survival "solution." A bunker can quickly become a tomb should some form of heavy debris from an explosion, fire, earthquake, or some other scenario cause the access and/or the air vents to become obstructed. Furthermore, some areas in the United States are susceptible to earthquake liquefaction, in which case, depending on the weight and displacement of the bunker (its density), it will either sink deeper into the earth and become totally buried or will literally float up into plain view. Either case is not good.

A remotely located bunker has some additional serious security risks, both short and long term. Its remote location alone makes covert access by thieves easy, and should it be found, it could be looted well before it is needed in an emergency. This is a legitimate concern, given that the contents of a bunker may not be insurable (which is not the case with a boat and its contents)—not to mention that if the theft went undiscovered, the bunker would be that much less able to support life. Another concern is that getting to a remote bunker before or in the immediate aftermath of a disaster might be difficult.

A bunker located beneath your home is more accessible but has its own set of adverse issues.

Few people realize that most underground bunkers have significant aboveground heat signatures from the bunker itself and from the exhaust systems that reach the surface—venting air, generator exhaust, sewage system ventilation, etc.). Some military bunkers utilize sophisticated countermeasures, but these are expensive and in most cases increase energy use. To prevent detection from infrared sensors, the temperature of all exhaust gases from the bunker must be adjusted to match the temperature outside the bunker at any given time. An alternative solution is to distribute the exhaust in minute amounts over a large area—hardly a practical solution for a home bunker.

Infrared technology is becoming quite inexpensive (some models cost less than $1,000) and increasingly ubiquitous. Anyone, with little or no training, can use a simple handheld infrared thermal imaging device and use it to find underground bunkers wherever they may be located. These same devices can also locate a man hiding in the woods, and some civilian models have that capability for both day and night. By using a solar rechargeable electric model airplane fitted with a basement model infrared device and minimal telemetry, an operator on the ground can even survey large areas for bunkers and personnel. It's easier than you might think. And should things get really tough, it's very possible that some survivors might turn on each other, while others may adapt a survival strategy of taking whatever they need from those who have.

Once a bunker is discovered, breaching it is easy: Find the vents using an infrared scanner, plug them, and the people inside come out. Getting their supplies is almost as easy as finding the bunker. And, as we all know, many unprepared survivors will be looking to survive by finding and taking the supplies of others. So, assuming they've had the foresight to equipment themselves with infrared technology, the strategic value of underground bunkers is less than you might think. I would guess that the gentlemen at some of the civilian-grade bunker manufacturing companies may not be making this disclosure to their clients.

Now let's compare the preceding with the security solution provided by a boat. Assume for the moment that you have a boat fully stocked with all kinds of the right stuff and it is in a slip or moored in a marina near a well-populated place somewhere on the coast of a large body of water. Let's limit this consideration to only the initial security situation from the onset of a catastrophic event and the next one to three days.

First, I believe that there are far better targets for the unprepared survivors right in town than any random boat. In other words, your boat is unlikely to be where anyone will look first. It will probably take a couple of days for survivors to clean out all of the stores, and by then anyone with a boat and a plan should be well on their way to their bug-out destination.

That's the worst-case scenario, in some situations, such as with a geomagnetic storm; you might have 18 to 24 hours advance warning before the event, which gives you ample time get your crew onboard and prepare to leave if the storm causes widespread damage to the national electrical grid and violence ensues.

Even supposing that a few people have intimate knowledge of your boat, such as where it is located and that it is well stocked with provisions, the likelihood that they will be in the right place at the right time to take advantage of all that information is low. Remember, many people will be displaced at the onset of most disasters, and transportation gridlock is a likely result of the kinds of infrastructure failures that can result from any number of credible disasters. (This includes many preppers, of course. They may end up trapped in a 10-mile-long line of cars stopped on some freeway along with a few thousand other panicked and hostile people.)

In addition, marinas, for the most part, are secured with security gates and fencing—as well as by fellow boaters, who don't want looters coming down on the docks any more than you would. So the odds of someone reaching your boat before you do is very limited. It is even less likely if you live aboard and work nearby, as many people who own larger sailboats do.

The probability of someone taking your boat, as opposed to just looting it, is even lower. I have been a licensed professional mariner for over 30 years, have accumulated over 150,000 miles at sea, and have operated all kinds of power- and sailboats. I am also a pilot with commercial multiengine instrument airplane and helicopter ratings. And I am considered an expert mechanic and electrician by my peers. Even if I wanted to steal a boat, I doubt that I could jump in and pull away from the dock as movies often depict—it's just not going to happen.

To take an unfamiliar boat to sea successfully, I would have to first take the time to familiarize myself with the vessel's controls and systems and the state of her readiness to put to sea. Imagine not knowing how much fuel was in the tanks and running out of fuel at the dock or a mile offshore (some boats use dipsticks for the tanks, not a gauge), or not knowing that a transmission shaft-lock was engaged, causing the engine to stall when placed in gear. Trying to steal an unknown vessel is very likely to end in failure. Don't believe everything you see in the movies! Even Navy Seals have to be specially trained on how to grab an unfamiliar vessel.

Anyone with even a little maritime experience would know this and would realize that stealing a boat that is unfamiliar is begging for disaster. Most people are not mariners, and those who could manage even a small vessel make up only a tiny percentage of the population—let alone a large trawler, sailboat, or long-range cruiser.

When we start looking at larger, long-range vessels, it's important to consider that they have layers of security that make them very "hard targets." Let's pretend for the moment that I wanted to steal one of the cruising sail or powerboats that I've worked on as a consultant. That work gave me intimate knowledge of the vessel, but to steal it I would still require a skilled crew (or at least one highly skilled partner) to work with me for at least hour to get under way—and that's assuming we boarded the ship undetected and knew exactly what to do as a team. While that's not impossible, it's far more likely to happen in a movie than in real life.

The bottom line is, under most circumstances, your boat is quite secure. If you are still concerned, speak with your mechanic and have him suggest and possibly diagram a way to covertly disable your engine such that even an experienced person would be baffled. You can also harden the vessel's access doors and hatches, making them more resistant to forced entry. Many doors and hatches I have created for clients and myself are also bullet resistant.

WEAPONS ONBOARD

The whole reason to have a boat, beyond recreational purposes, is to save yourself, your family, and friends from the dangers that follow an initial disaster by sailing away well before civil violence begins. And if you can avoid that threat, then you may not need firearms. I don't believe it's mandatory to carry firearms onboard your vessel, but it's a personal decision each captain must make.

If you do decide to carry firearms, some are better suited than others. For example, the following weapons are very resistant to corrosion (rust) and useful for both hunting and defense:

- Mossberg 500 Special Purpose Mariner (stainless steel) 12-gauge shotgun with 20-inch barrel
- Ruger model 10/22 stainless steel .22 caliber carbine with synthetic stock
- Marlin Papoose .22 caliber rifle model 70PSS stainless steel break-down model

It is critically important to review the local laws of any country where you plan to sail if you have any firearms, ammunition, or other weapons onboard and comply with those laws—or accept the risk of violating them. In many countries it's illegal to carry any firearms onboard your boat. In Mexico, for example, if you are boarded by authorities during a routine inspection and they find even one bullet, they can seize your boat and put you in prison! It's no joke. Deviation from local laws in the event of a worldwide or localized disaster is a calculated risk you must consider.

Some items aboard your vessel can serve dual duty, working for their original purposes as well as defense, and they are legal to carry onboard in any country. I believe these items make the most sense, because they have utility, whether or not you need to use them as a lethal defensive weapon.

Flare Pistols

The USCG requires that vessels 16 feet in length and above carry a complement of signaling devices, which must also include any combination of a total of three day/night approved red flares, which can be aerial (rocket-flare or launched from a pistol) and/or handheld. Keep in mind that this is the required *minimum*, which in my opinion is not optimal; I like to carry a dozen or more signaling flares and signaling devices. The U.S. Coast Guard maintains a list of the specific safety requirements for vessels based upon type, use, and number of passengers onboard at their website, www.uscgboating.org. I strongly encourage everyone who owns, operates, or crews on a boat to visit this website and gain familiarity with the USCG safety requirements, which do change from time to time.

In an emergency life-threatening situation, many legal marine-grade flare pistols can be used effectively at close range as a deterrent against potential threats and unwelcome boarders. These flare pistols can be purchased without any permit or license by anyone over the age of 18.

Orion manufactures several lightweight, and easy-to-carry and –operate models. Trust me, when a criminal is looking down the barrel of a 25mm flare pistol he will quickly forget whatever dumb scheme he had planned. These pistols can be deadly at close range and can inflict a very serious injury at 10 yards or more, and they have a vertical range of about 375 feet when fired.

Flare pistols are readily available at any marine supply store and are available in both 12 gauge and 25mm calibers. I prefer the larger, 25mm pistol for a couple reasons:

1. In an emergency it's a superior signaling device.
2. As a defensive weapon in a life-threatening situation, the 25mm flare pistol is formidable!

I encourage you to have several of these pistols onboard for both signaling and in case of any life-threatening situations for defensive purposes. The 12-gauge pistol is smaller and lighter than the 25mm pistol; as a defensive weapon, it is suited for older children who are properly trained in its use.

Sometimes when my wife and I are in remote areas and hiking on land away from our boat I will carry a 12-gauge flare pistol tucked in my belt, with an extra pistol and rounds in my backpack, as an added security measure.

Spear Guns

A diver's spear gun is another great defensive weapon, as well as being handy for shooting large fish in shallow water. They come in two basic types: models that are operated by stretched surgical tubing and pneumatic models that are pumped or use a compressed air (CO_2) cartridge.

A spear gun is a deadly weapon at close range, and that's no joke! Spear guns are designed to skewer and kill large fish underwater at ranges of 10 to 12 feet, so when one is discharged above water the spear has a much greater velocity, and therefore even greater range—if the spear is not tethered to the gun. I have tested the tubing-type spear guns on land and have impaled solid wooden targets 20 feet away.

Pellet Rifles

I also recommend carrying at least one .22 caliber pellet rifle. Even in Mexico, where the laws on possessing firearms are arguably extreme, you can legally posses a pellet rifle. In fact, in Mexico you can buy one in almost any hardware or marine supply store, legally.

The new-technology hand-cocked, piston-powered pellet rifles (made by Gammo) that are now available have amazing power and accuracy. Some newer-model pellet rifles have muzzle velocities of 1,200 feet per second, which approximates the muzzle velocity of a .22 caliber rifle cartridge using gunpowder, and they are relatively quiet when discharged. These pellet rifles are great for both hunting and for use as a defensive weapon. Some better models are equipped with scopes, since they have a maximum effective range of 50 yards.

The ammunition for these rifles consists of a small lead pellet (the bullet), which does not require any gunpowder since it is propelled by compressed air generated by the rifle. These pellets are relatively inexpensive and take up very little space. It would be easy to carry 5,000 pellets sealed in a glass jelly jar or tea tin.

Hunting Bows

Compound bows and crossbows are also legal to possess in most countries onboard a vessel and also provide dual duty for hunting and defensive utility. A bow can be used to hunt game on land and, with an optional spool of line, can be used to shoot large fish. Both types of bows are deadly, have effective ranges as long as 50 yards, and are relatively silent. Where those qualities are required, a bow is very effective.

Machetes

A machete is great to have when you are hiking in dense brush or jungle environments. It can also double as an excellent defensive weapon to repel unauthorized boarders who have no firearms. I usually equip my expedition boats with several machetes since they are legal to possess in most countries. They are also great for barter worldwide.

Baseball Bats

Aluminum baseball bats are great for subduing large fish when you bring them on deck. They can double as excellent defensive weapons and can be used effectively to repel boarders who do not have firearms or those armed with machetes. Baseball bats are legal in most countries.

Slingshots

Modern slingshots have incredible power, especially if you use small ball bearings as shot. They can be used effectively at distances up to 50 feet. You can use them to hunt small game or to repel boarders or pirates who have no firearms. Slingshots are easy to carry in a backpack and are legal in most countries. I usually have several onboard just for fun. They are also great for barter.

BUILDING IN SECURITY

How you go about adding shielding and other security features, or *hardening*, your boat, depends on whether you are building from scratch, buying a used boat, or modifying a boat you already own, as well as on the boat's primary construction material: steel, aluminum, fiberglass, or wood. Steel boats are much easier to harden than the others, as you might expect.

All boats need reinforced windows and doors with extremely strong hinges and locking mechanisms. Doors should be steel plate mounted in a steel frame. Windows should be set into bronze or heavy-gauge aluminum frame sets (or steel frames for steel-hulled boats) and should be made of at least ½-inch-thick abrasion-resistant polycarbonate plastic. Whether you are building or retrofitting, you will need to hire a ballistics consultant to establish exact thicknesses for materials to ensure resistance to bullets, shrapnel, and other flying debris.

Fuel tanks and machinery spaces may also need protection to suit your needs; be sure to collaborate with an experienced consultant.

Hardening a New Boat

If you are building a boat, you will be able to accomplish a more elegant hardening of the vessel than if you are retrofitting an existing boat.

Discuss the concept of hardening your vessel with the builder from your very first conversation because it will affect the construction methods (as well as the cost). With steel construction the costs of hardening will likely be less than that of using steel and Kevlar in a wooden or fiberglass vessel.

A steel boat also presents the absolute best solution as a survival vessel from the standpoint of durability and resistance to small arms fire, shrapnel, and the flying debris seen in hurricanes and tornados. Hardening of a steel vessel in selected key areas simply involves using heavier plating in those areas. The performance of a properly designed vessel will not suffer from being hardened.

Hardening an Existing Boat

If you're modifying an existing vessel—especially if you are a "do-it-yourself" kind of prepper—adding security features might be an interesting challenge. However, depending on the material used in the construction of your boat, the challenge can be significant. Fiberglass and wooden boats will be much harder to retrofit with the enhancements needed, and in the end, only certain areas of the vessel can be actually hardened, leaving many spaces above and below decks vulnerable. That said, judiciously used steel plates and woven Kevlar can add significant and meaningful areas of protection. The areas that should be considered for hardening include the hull and bulkheads (walls) around mission-critical systems such as:

- Batteries and electronics
- Fuel and water tanks
- Engine and machinery spaces
- Safety zones for personnel

If you're lucky enough to already own a steel boat, then, depending on how important aesthetics are to you, you can easily weld on reinforcing plates to the exterior where added protection is needed. If it needs to look pretty, then you'll have to install plates on the inside of the hull in those areas, which is more work. In cases where that is impossible, you can use Kevlar, though it is more expensive.

If you have concerns about hostile encounters, then protection levels up to and including all .30 caliber rifle rounds may be prudent. If you're up against a .50 caliber weapon, odds are you will sustain damage until you are out of range unless you have 1-inch hardened plating. Here again, the key to survival is to avoid conflict by maintaining situational awareness and taking evasive action well in advance of anticipated risks (see the following section).

Just for reference, although most supertanker hulls are about 1-inch-thick steel, in comparison to a 50- to 70-foot steel sailboat with a hull made of ⅜-inch plate steel, the supertanker is far less robust. A supertanker loaded with oil might have a total mass equal to 300,000 tons, so when its inch-thick hull hits a rock, it cracks like an eggshell due to the relatively high loading pressure (pounds per square inch, or PSI). By comparison, the PSI of a 40- to 90-ton boat with a thinner hull would be far less, allowing the hull to simply "bounce off" the rock.

Aluminum is softer than steel and more easily penetrated by projectiles, rocks, and other hard objects. Therefore, they also need significant hardening in all critical areas. In doing so, great care must be taken to avoid electrolysis when steel and aluminum are in close proximity to each other in the presence of seawater. Electrolysis occurs when you place dissimilar metals in close proximity to each other in the presence of an electrolyte, such as seawater, forming what is essentially a battery cell, which causes the associated less-noble metals to be eroded over time.

The best advice for using various grades of steel in and around aluminum boats can be obtained from shipyards that do a lot of construction with aluminum. It may be permissible in some interior areas to use 316-grade stainless steel plating. Layers of Kevlar can also be safely used on the inside, as well as stainless steel, although it is expensive. Kevlar must be installed properly, so before proceeding consult with the manufacturer or a qualified ballistics expert.

FEATURES THAT FACILITATE OPERATIONAL TACTICS

Hardening your vessel is all very well and good, but the tactics you employ if you ever come under fire by armed pirates, domestic or foreign, are what may save your life.

If your vessel comes under attack by armed pirates, you'll want to present them with the smallest possible target by steering directly away from them—or directly into them. Stern-on or bow-on position presents the smallest vessel profile and, as such, the smallest target for aggressors, so you may want to give the bow and stern some additional attention in the hardening process. Given these areas are comparatively small, it may make sense to use heavier armor in there. Given that the bow of our current vessel is reinforced to deal with impacts from thin ice pack, it should work well in the event we need to ram a hostile vessel. The bow and stern areas also have a secondary collision bulkhead made of ½-inch steel plate.

The combined thickness of the outer and inner layers of steel is over ¾ of an inch thick.

On some past vessels I have also installed sharpened cutting surfaces (heavy industrial serrated edges) at and below the waterline at the bow, such that if the boat passes over a large line or drift net at sea, the line or netting will be cut before it reaches the stern. This prevents the propeller or rudder from getting fouled by lines and nets. There are thousands of lost lines and nets floating at or near the surface of the oceans worldwide, and sometimes pirates intentionally stretch a polypropylene line (which floats) across several miles of ocean to trap vessels that are motoring by disabling their propulsion.

Once your propeller is tangled up with a big ball of poly line it's useless, and the boat slows to a stop, making it more vulnerable to attack. In some cases the ball of poly line will wrap around the propeller to the point where it will jam against the hull or support strut, and this can cause enough friction to damage the vessel's transmission—which is not a good thing. If you ever get a line or net caught in your propeller, you'll need a large, super sharp serrated bread knife and a mask and fins to clear it off the propeller.

The bridge or tiller area should be secured, if possible. If it isn't, you should consider installing a forward-looking camera system, such as those used as backup cameras on large buses and recreational vehicles, combined with a remote controller for the autopilot. With this equipment, you can operate your vessel while remaining below decks in a hardened safe zone deep inside your boat.

ELECTRONIC SHIELDING

All boats should have their electronics systems shielded against damage from all forms of electromagnetic interference, including lightning and the E1/E2 emissions from an electromagnetic pulse (EMP). An EMP can be generated by a high-altitude nuclear detonation, also known as HEMP, and vessels should be protected to the maximum extent possible. Some of the modern military vessels also have short-range EMP weapons, which have the same adverse effects on electronic equipment. Metal vessels offer more intrinsic protection for electronic gear than those made of fiberglass or wood. This is because any metal that is between the high-energy E1/E2 HEMP emissions and the electronics inside the boat will tend to attenuate the strength of the damaging E1/E2 energy, thus helping to protect the equipment, assuming other countermeasures are in place to protect wiring systems to and from electronics, including antennas. Simply speaking, metal boats are imperfect Faraday cages, but can be significantly enhanced. On the other hand, materials that are transparent to radio frequency emissions such as wood and fiberglass cannot shield any device from the HEMP emissions and provide no protection whatsoever.

Hardening a boat's electronics against HEMP or a lightning strike, which has an energy discharge similar to the "E2" phase of an electromagnetic pulse, is a matter best left to an experienced electrical engineer with training in EMI shielding, as it is well beyond the know-how of some boat builders, naval architects, and marine electricians. Trust me: It's much more than just grounding everything!

SURVEILLANCE AND ALARM SYSTEMS

You should also consider several types of alarm systems for use on your boat.

Bilge Alarms

High-water alarms use what is called a float switch, wired to an audible alarm horn. A backup horn like that used on delivery trucks is ideal for this purpose, and you can build a simple yet highly reliable water alarm that will sound off at 105 decibels if you have any water intrusion into the bilge of your boat. Secure the float switch, which can be purchased at any marine supply store, to the lowest point in the boat's bilge. There are two wires coming from the float switch that are connected in series with the positive supply (wire) from a 12 VDC power source (B+)—protect the B+ wire with a fuse suitable to the current used by the alarm horn—and the positive terminal on the alarm horn. The negative terminal from the alarm horn connects to the negative ground bus (-12VDC).

The alarm will sound when water enters the boat. The switch floats up and triggers the contacts that allow the current from the B+ wire to flow into the horn alarm. In the old days, they used a mercury contact in the float switch, which was actually more reliable than a mechanically operated switch, but thanks to environmental regulations that awesome switch is hard to find.

Door and Hatch Alarms

Most electrical supply stores sell wireless home alarm equipment and systems. These systems have door switches that operate on discrete FM frequencies, and when a magnetic contact is interrupted, it triggers a tiny transmitter that's built into the switch to send a signal to the alarm system, which sets off the alarm. Your choice of audible or silent alarm and/or strobe lights can be wired to go off, causing everyone within a few hundred yards to take notice.

You can also wire a cell phone dialer to the system so that should any switch go off (water intrusion alarm, door or hatch opened, smoke, fire, CO_2, engine starting, etc.) it calls a preprogrammed phone number. In place of (or in addition to) the cell phone dialer, you can use what is called a page-alert system that will beep a pager that you carry should any alarm switch be activated.

The page-alert system uses a compact transmitter that operates on an AM frequency near the Citizens' Band radio frequencies and has a range of about 5 miles from the boat. This is a standalone system (doesn't require any outside services, so in post-disaster situations, it will still function, assuming it was protected from any initial damage). It also allows you to be beeped if, say, you are away from your boat in the wilderness or on some tropical island collecting coconuts and something starts to go wrong back onboard the boat.

Cameras and Motion Alarms

With the advent of wireless digital cameras that work day or night, it's very easy to install surveillance cameras around your vessel and have them send live feeds to a recorder or your computer or smart phone in real time. They can also be wired to be triggered remotely or to start taking photos when a motion sensor sets them off, and those photos can be sent the same as video so you can see what's going on at your boat at any moment in time—even if you are halfway around the world!

Some of these systems can be integrated into a burglar alarm system that is programmed to call the police directly, as well as send the photographic data, thereby speeding the capture of any ill-fated bad guys. This kind of system is great for protecting your boat prior to any disaster event.

Radar Alarms

When you are at anchor in a remote location, your radar system will become important to helping you to maintain your situational awareness. If I feel we are in an area where someone could possibly approach our vessel at anchor, I run the radar at night. In some cases I also run it during the day, since it can "see" approaching objects much farther away than any human, even beyond the horizon.

The Furuno radars (I like having two units) we use have a maximum range of 50 miles, and some models have much longer ranges. You can set the radar to sound an alarm anytime a target gets closer than the allowable distance you have preselected. A connection on the back of the radar unit allows the use of various external alarms: strobe light or the type of truck back-up horn discussed above, which emits a 110 decibel alarm easily heard for 100 yards in any direction. Using radar this way protects you against incursions from anyone but U.S. Navy Seals. These radar units are so sensitive they can detect sea lions on the surface of the water!

CHAPTER 6
Escape and Survive

The survival and escape tactics meaningful for people who are using a sailboat for relocation, shelter, and survival are somewhat different than what would be employed by people following other survival paradigms, although some similarities exist. Nautical prepping provides a unique survival strategy, which is supported by tactical options that are not available with other survival paradigms. Regardless of the survival strategy employed, situational awareness can make all the difference. However, in particular situations, as discussed later in the chapter, the disaster itself will determine and shape the landscape of available options at any given time, many of which may not be available to terrestrial preppers. Whereby using a boat, which may also happen to be your home, allows you to expediently bug out and potentially save yourself and all your preps along with some or possibly all of your personal belongings. On the other hand, terrestrial preppers who are sheltering in place and may at some point be forced to relocate for one reason or another will not have that option, and will likely be limited to bug out with only whatever they can carry in a backpack (bug-out bag).

Being able to almost instantly relocate your entire household hundreds and even thousands of miles away from any disaster-related risks and to areas with better resources for living is strategically superior to most other plans of action. Unfortunately, terrestrial preppers who attempt to relocate anytime post-disaster will be faced with hazardous overland travel, which will be very difficult, thereby limiting the achievable relocation distance possible.

The Importance of Situational Awareness

Situational awareness—knowing what's going on as early as possible during an impending disaster—is key to making a timely risk assessment in a specific disaster scenario. Some disasters can be predicted with great accuracy and with significant lead time. Hurricanes, for example, provide ample time to make critical tactical decisions. The National Oceanic and Atmospheric Administration (NOAA) provides a host of reporting services that can be accessed using your radio equipment and through the National Hurricane Center online at http://www.nhc.noaa.gov.

NOAA also provides real-time weather casting via weather radio, which includes localized forecasting services on frequencies that can be received by all VHF radio receivers and transceivers.

Using the information provided by NOAA and others, boat owners who keep their boats in marinas or at other coastal locations can have several days' advance warning of any potential landfall of serious weather events such as hurricanes—although, interestingly, in such events many owners take little heed of oncoming adverse weather events.

In the case of Hurricane Katrina, for example, there was more than ample time for boat owners to safely secure or relocate their boats dozens of miles inland on the local rivers, bays, and inlets, far away from the damaging winds, seas, and tides that impacted the coastal marinas. However, few boat owners took the initiative to protect their boats.

I can only speculate about the reasons for this lack of action, based upon my own general observations and logic. I would guess that, because most boat owners have insurance coverage on their boats, they feel protected in that way. It is also likely that people tend to prioritize other responsibilities such as jobs, homes, and families over movable property like a boat. And, of course, some people probably just decide to wait and see what happens.

In any case, many boats suffer preventable damage in these storms. Even something as simple as adding additional dock lines can keep boats from breaking loose, crashing into pilings and other boats, and being irreparably damaged. Boats that break loose pose serious hazards to all the other boats around them as they are driven about by high winds, waves, and storm surge. Many boats that would have otherwise survived a storm fall victim to their unsecured neighbors.

I believe that boats belonging to preppers will not suffer this fate because those owners have a bigger investment and commitment, both financially and psychologically, in the preservation of their vessels because their survival paradigms rely on these boats. Preppers who have prepared a sailboat as a survival platform can and should opt to relocate their boats to a safer location well in advance of a hurricane making landfall, thereby eliminating or greatly minimizing the damage to their vessels. I would go so far as to speculate that once marine insurance underwriters become aware of nautical preppers, they might even consider offering special rates to preppers for their boats. A proactive owner such as this will surely reduce the losses incurred over time by any insurance carrier.

In fact, preppers with adequate situational awareness will assess any oncoming event, be it a forecast tsunami, where there may be as much as 5 to 6 hours' warning, or a hurricane, where there may be as much as several days' advance warning, and take preplanned steps and options to relocate themselves and their vessel out of harm's way.

Specific Disaster Scenarios

Just so there is no confusion, I am not predicting the end of the world or implying that anything in particular is going to happen. I am by nature a bit of a skeptic with a background in science and industrial arts. I am a believer in math and statistical inference and employ those methods in considering and weighing the potential odds and risks associated with everyday activities, financial investments, and even with the potential reoccurrence of the various disasters that have actually been observed and recorded during the past 200 years. I am not interested in plans or exercises that deal with the potential for risks due to rarely occurring events such as polar shifts, impact with near earth objects, eruption of super volcanoes, and other such events that may reoccur on schedules that more closely relate to the time-cycles of geologic events, which happen every few thousand years or more.

Personally, I am more concerned about credible potential risks stemming from natural and man-caused disasters that have average occurrence cycles of every 100 years or less, such as severe geomagnetic storms, which occur on average roughly every 30 years, or major hurricanes that can strike as often as every 5 years. So with that in mind, let's take a look at some disaster scenarios and the solutions that I believe may be relevant to those events. We also must consider the very real potential for a man-caused disaster that might be related to some form of nuclear, biological, or conventional warfare.

Let's start by considering some actual and proposed tactics that may be employed in certain disaster scenarios. Obviously the tactics employed for local and regional-scale disasters, which may not have long durations, are different than those tactics employed for large scale, continental, or global disasters that would likely be of long duration as a result of secondary effects; i.e. loss of critical infrastructure and the breakdown of society and violent competition for resources, resulting in a world without the rule of law.

TSUNAMI

When I lived in Hawaii, when a tsunami was forecast, mariners such as myself simply took our vessels off the docks and moorings and sailed out into deep water—where a tsunami has no noticeable effect—and safely waited out its passing. Once it passed, we would return to our docks and moorings.

Simply speaking, if you take your boat into water that is deeper than 300 feet or so (the deeper the better), you won't have to worry about a breaking wave crushing down on your boat. The surge of the water isn't a problem when you are a mile or two offshore, since the real danger is being carried onshore and crashing into hard objects there. Of course, if you aren't able to get your boat out before a tsunami hits, then a steel boat will fare better than others, since it will be robust enough to handle being slammed around.

HURRICANE

As suggested above, of the boats that are lost and damaged due to hurricanes, nearly all are at or near their slips at a marina. Conversely, most boats caught at sea in hurricanes survive with minimal damage.

The reason so many boats are lost in the marina are twofold: The effects of storm are more intense in shallow water because breaking waves, tidal surges, and high winds combine to drive boats into each other. And, as mentioned, many owners don't properly secure their boats.

As always, the key to preparedness is having a plan in place well before you need it. In case of the planning for an approaching hurricane, while the weather is still nice and you have ample time (now would be good), make a careful survey of the local charts, noting all the nearby rivers and protected bays and inlets that are navigable by your vessel. Once you have made that survey, make a trip with your boat to each of these spots, going as far upriver or into the bay or inlet as possible, and make notes on the locations where your vessel can make anchor (using several anchors) and that afford the greatest protection from the effects of the storm—and other boats.

The key concept in anchoring in protected waters is to locate the vessel where there is minimal *fetch*—the distance over water where wind-driven waves can build. Basically, at any given wind speed, the greater the fetch, the larger the wind waves will become. The books on seamanship listed in Chapter 3 detail the effects of fetch and offer detailed plans on building a storm mooring. Sometimes you can even use fixed objects onshore to secure lines to and from your vessel, thereby stabilizing it from moving as a result of high winds, which are usually the main issue in protected waters during a storm. Keep in mind that as the storm moves through the area, the direction of the winds will shift, so you want to secure the boat from as many directions as possible.

Once the storm passes, if damage to the area was significant, as it was in Katrina, you can continue to remain on your boat at the storm mooring. It will provide a secure shelter away from the conflict and strife that may exist in the more densely populated areas, and you can quietly wait it out until things stabilize.

A position out on the water is far more defensible than most locations on land. People wanting to reach you would be forced to swim, or use a small boat, in which case, they can be repelled as needed. If your location becomes overly compromised, you can pull anchor at that point and sail out to sea and to a new location beyond the areas affected by the hurricane and make port where there is no strife.

PANDEMIC DISEASE OR BIOLOGICAL ATTACK

The tactics that can be employed in the event of a pandemic disease, such as a flu epidemic, are relatively simple. Before you are exposed or quarantined by government authorities, quickly move your family and other loved ones onboard your boat and relocate to a more inaccessible location.

Even if the disease is highly contagious, being several hundred yards or a mile offshore will provide adequate physical distance to ensure safety from exposure. Initially, this location may simply be a short distance offshore, up a river, on a protected bay or inlet, or anchored just offshore, assuming the weather is fair. You can also hoist a yellow "quarantine flag," which is in and of itself a deterrent to others since it means there are sick people onboard the vessel. Under maritime laws, this flag alone should be enough to keep all other boaters away from your vessel. From this isolated location you can initially observe how things are progressing onshore by monitoring your radios.

If you feel that some or all of your crew may have suffered some exposure, you can start by using various naturopathic immunity boosters such as olive leaf extract. However, it would be best to consult with a naturopathic doctor for the most comprehensive advice as to what immunity boosters would be advised and best kept in your onboard medical kit. You can also consider using any antiviral (like Tamiflu) or other prophylactic medications in your first-aid/medical kit that are indicated for use in the given situation by your family physician, following, of course, the instructions you have from your physician for the use of those prescription drugs.

Using your communications equipment, you can safely collect information on the progression and status of any pandemic by monitoring FEMA radio and the Emergency Broadcast System messages, as well as any other news broadcasts and civilian communications on CB and VHF radio.

Depending upon the outcome of events onshore and the duration of those events, you can modify your tactics accordingly. If the event turns out to be short lived, then once all the cases of illness have cleared and FEMA, the Centers for Disease Control, or other authorities have indicated that the risk has passed, you can return to your land base at your convenience.

If for some reason the event is long lasting with secondary effects that create a situation where the rule of law has ceased to apply and violence has taken over, you can use your option to relocate far offshore to a preplanned destination, as discussed in Chapter 1.

MAJOR EARTHQUAKE

Boats floating on water don't "feel" the effects of earthquakes. Many boaters who were onboard their boats in the San Francisco Bay during the 7.0 magnitude 1989 earthquake reported that they didn't feel anything. However, an earthquake of sufficient magnitude can devastate any major city to the point where it becomes uninhabitable. As with other regional and localized natural disasters, it will take time—perhaps a long time—before outside help arrives and restores order and services. In the meantime, bad things can and do happen, as we saw in the aftermath of Hurricane Katrina.

In the case of a major earthquake, the plan would be to get your family and loved ones onboard as quickly as possible, and then relocate your boat as you would in the case of a pandemic disease—offshore and away from the risks of fire, explosions, falling debris, and irrational people. From this relatively isolated location, you can safely and comfortably follow the aftermath of such a devastating event using your onboard radio equipment.

In this case, it's likely that after a few weeks or months, the efforts of outside help will have achieved the desired effect and any lawlessness will have been neutralized. At this point, you can continue to comfortably live onboard your boat until such time as a better housing situation presents itself. However, compared to a well-equipped sailboat, that situation may be a long time in the making.

NUCLEAR ATTACK

In my opinion, this is one of the more grave scenarios because of the large number of initial casualties from the actual explosion, related structural damage and fires, and radiation poisoning near ground zero and from downwind fallout.

If you and your boat are far enough from ground zero to survive the initial attack, you have several options.

As in other scenarios, everyone needs to follow your family's emergency plan of action to reach the boat as quickly as possible. The boat needs to then relocate to an area upwind from ground zero to avoid the fallout.

I don't profess to be an expert on radiation; however, you will need to decontaminate passengers as they board and before they go inside the boat. This requires that they remove and discard all their clothing overboard and wash down using clean water and soap. Once someone is decontaminated they can then move inside the boat, find their stored clothing, and get dressed. After everyone is decontaminated, the boat should get under way.

If an isolated location upwind of ground zero is not feasible, then you should set a course tangential to the direction of the fallout heading downwind. Anyone who comes on deck from down below to assist in vessel operations should wear a full set of rubber foul-weather gear and boots, which must both be diligently washed before they are taken back below decks, to avoid carrying contamination into the living quarters. Assume that radio-active contamination is present on all external surfaces and act accordingly; that will help ensure the safety of everyone onboard.

Once the boat is removed from close proximity to shore and any additional exposure risks, you will need to clean and decontaminate the exterior of the boat as thoroughly as possible using seawater (or freshwater if you are in a lake or river) and soap.

Once you have completed the decontamination of the people onboard and the boat itself, you'll want to administer any oral antidotes and prophylactic medications for radiation poisoning that you have onboard. Potassium iodide, diethylenetriamine pentaacetic acid (DTPA), and Prussian blue are all used for radiation sickness—be sure to obtain instructions in their use by a qualified doctor before laying in these supplies. Mariners on early nuclear submarines also ate bananas and drank red wine, which provided some mild ongoing prophylactic protection from radiation.

At this point, the immediate issues have been addressed, so you must begin to assess the situation to determine the appropriate next steps. You will certainly want to remain as isolated as possible, keeping a very close watch on the wind and weather so that you don't suddenly end up downwind from ground zero if the wind changes direction.

The first logical question will concern the scale the nuclear attack. Was the detonation a single isolated event or part of a widespread attack? The reason for gathering this information is critical to your next step, which is to get out of danger. You don't want to sail toward another area that was also hit by a nuclear weapon.

In this scenario, if the event was an isolated attack, then you can sail to somewhere upwind or far away on tangential course from the direction of the path of the fallout. This may involve a voyage of several hundred miles or more, but that shouldn't be any problem for a properly prepared sailboat. And once you have arrived at an unaffected location, you and your crewmembers can seek medical care as needed.

If the nuclear attack is a large-scale event and many cities have been attacked, then you will have to employ your offshore plan and sail to a chosen remote island or location for an extended stay.

LARGE-SCALE, CONTINENTAL, OR GLOBAL DISASTER

As I discussed at the beginning of the book, there are several types of large-scale, continental, or global disasters and events that can pose very real and credible risks to modern civilization.

Such large-scale events include an international pandemic, severe geomagnetic storms, high-altitude electromagnetic pulse weapons, and of course global nuclear war. The operational tactics for sailing preppers vary somewhat with each scenario; however, in the event of any such large-scale disaster, the options for loitering nearby your homeport and waiting for some resolution are likely fruitless. Therefore, in such an event, you will likely have to head far offshore to a predetermined safe location and set up for long-term survival.

This is where a sailboat really shines, since it combines the features of a long-range bug-out vehicle and a secure shelter that happens to carry all your gear and supplies. It also has the unique capacity to relocate you and your loved ones to a favorable survival location that will be inaccessible to others, thereby greatly reducing the odds of being on the receiving end of deadly violence and increasing your odds for survival.

Closing Thoughts

Both preppers and sailors hope for best, but the wise and experienced prepare for the worst. I believe the paradigm described in this book will put you in a superior situation to people who have spent the time and money to have a bunker built and installed—especially one in a remote location. In the worst case, you can be out sailing in the sun with your family and friends, having a great time. And if you're feeling truly adventurous, you can visit that island you have selected just for fun.

However, all of this is just my personal opinion. I strongly urge anyone undertaking *any* plan, strategy, or action to first conduct extensive due diligence in concert with their own advisors and experts. I wish everyone the very best of luck regardless of their prepper paradigm. Let's all hope and pray we never need to use any of these preparations.

Wishing you fair winds and seas, sunny days, and starlit nights!

Captain William E. Simpson II
United States Merchant Marine

APPENDIX A:
Sailboat Examples

The following examples illustrate the principles discussed in the "Sailboats" section of Chapter 2. If you are new to sailing, you may find you need to do some study before these descriptions will make sense, as they rely on common sailing terminology and concepts.

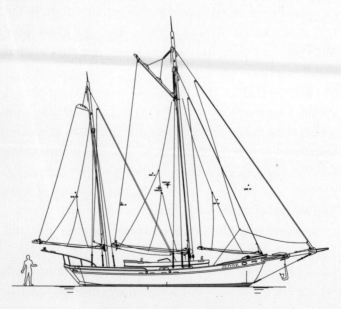

Side view, sailboat *Zephyr*

The 42-foot ketch *Zephyr* was designed after a rough passage along the West Coast of the United States. The *Zephyr*'s rig is a gaff ketch, which has the advantages of offering many perfectly balanced sail combinations while keeping the sail aspect ratio within bounds.

The hull, deck, and house structures are steel. Bowsprit, masts, and booms are all aluminum pipe for the sake of lightness, strength, economy, and ease of fabrication, repair, and maintenance.

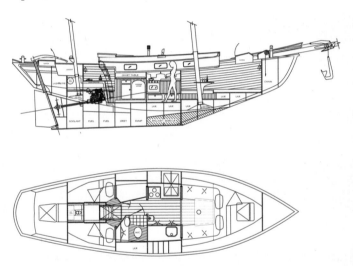

Interior side and top views of the *Zephyr*

The *Zephyr*'s interior layout is optimized for a couple with two guests. This is a good layout for three onboard for a passage, with two living aboard most of the time. A pair of single berths are located aft, for sleeping in rough weather or to accommodate occasional guests. The galley is large and centrally located. The sitting/dining area, galley, and forward v-berth together comprise the living and entertainment area. There is plenty of deck space for lounging, while the cockpit is small so it can be emptied quickly if it fills with green water.

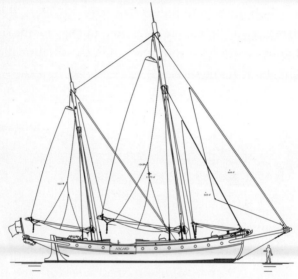

Sailboat *Asgard*

Here we have the 66-foot ketch *Asgard*. It has flush decks in the ends, which would help it survive a rollover and right itself without incident. The cockpit, being central, is protected from boarding seas coming from aft. It is also self-draining, with its sole well above the waterline. Ample deck area provides storage for shore boats and other gear.

A true motor vessel engine was specified for the *Asgard*, in combination with sufficient tank capacity for 4,000 nautical miles under power alone. Of course, since it is a fully functional sailboat, its range is effectively unlimited.

The ketch sail rig was chosen for its flexibility and balance. I would call the sail rig a Bermuda ketch due to the raked masts, loose-footed sails, and headboards aloft. The reason the rig is arranged this way is so that the sails can be laced onto the masts rather than requiring expensive yacht hardware.

The hull and decks are all steel. The hull draft is less than six feet, so the boat will fit anywhere outside the one fathom line on charts. The shoal keel also would allow you to beach the boat to clean the bottom at low tide — which is a common strategy among the work boats of the world. The masts are schedule 40 aluminum pipe, selected for its extreme ruggedness, simplicity, ease of fabrication, and minimum maintenance requirements.

Because *Asgard* is a double-ended boat it has perfect balance when heeled, and it's fast:

11.5 knots under sail to as much as 12 knots downwind with a following sea. Believe me, 40-some tons of boat blasting along at 12 knots under sail is definitely something to write home about!

Side and top interior views of the *Asgard*

Compared to the 42-foot *Zephyr*, the *Asgard* is quite a large boat. With a king-size berth in each of the staterooms, the layout is perfect for two couples to permanently live aboard or cruise the oceans of the world. There are accommodations for two additional crew members, adults or youths.

For the day guests or crew, there is a third head compartment complete with shower. It would accommodate occasional guests very nicely, or extra crew on a long voyage. It could even be arranged as another private stateroom.

Aft of the head is a navigator's station, and the boat has two very generous socializing areas: one below and one on deck. The galley is quite large, although most of the time meals would be eaten on deck in the center cockpit. Naturally, it would be simple to arrange a Bimini cover for shade and rain protection.

Asgard is my ideal permanent live-aboard sailboat, bar none.

APPENDIX B:
Motorsailer Examples

The 42-foot motor sailing yacht *Lucille* lives up to the criteria described in the "Motorsailing Boats" section on page 47 nicely.

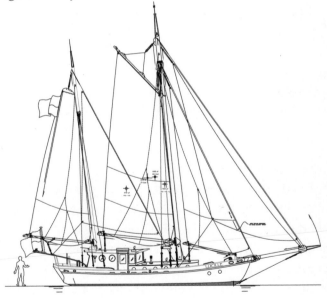

Side view of the *Lucille*

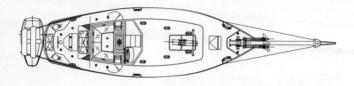

Top deck view of *Lucille*

These plans above reveal a unique combination of sailboat and motor yacht: fully enclosed pilot house, fully capable engine and sail rig combined with a sailing hull.

A fully feathering controllable-pitch propeller system (manufactured by Nogva of Norway) allows ultimate flexibility when motoring, motor sailing, or just sailing with the propeller feathered to the slipstream.

A ketch rig was chosen for its flexibility and balance (see Appendix A for more on this), and the sail area is the same as that of a sailboat, so there is no lack of performance when the wind blows.

Because the *Lucille* was designed for the European canal system, the masts fold down easily, and to conserve dockside fees the bowsprit hinges up, greatly reducing overall length. The pilot house is quite low for the sake of minimum windage but also to clear the canal system's height limits. Inside, the pilot house has all the accoutrements of a motor yacht. *Lucille* even has two steering stations: one inside for motor yacht mode and one outside for the fun of sailing.

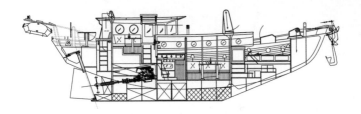

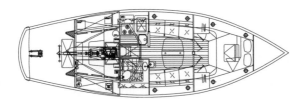

Side and top interior views of the *Lucille*

The interior of the *Lucille* has been optimized for a couple to cruise onboard for long voyages, but it is also highly capable as a full-time live-aboard yacht. There is a king-size berth forward in its own private suite. The rest of the space below is occupied by a generous socializing area, with dining table, a snug galley for offshore safety, and a head with shower.

In the pilot house, a dinette is arranged so that when you are seated you can see out forward and to the sides. The aft deck has a wraparound seat, and there is an additional seat on the aft side of the pilot house.

Is this the ideal survival boat for two people? Probably.

Let's consider a larger option, in case there are more than two of you bugging out.

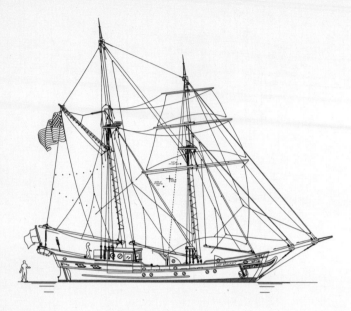

Side view of the *Mermaid*

This is the 62-foot motor sailing cargo/passenger yacht *Mermaid*. Originally conceived as a cargo boat for small packets in the Caribbean, as of this writing the *Mermaid* is a day charter boat for sail training in the Chesapeake Bay.

She has an all-steel structure for hull, deck, and house, with schedule 40 aluminum pipe for spars. The rig is a classic brigantine, which is possibly the best all-around rig for cruising and for long-range voyaging.

Without the square sails, the vessel can be tacked to windward. With the two square topsails the same can be accomplished in all but heavy winds. The lower square sail is merely a running sail for light weather—or speed.

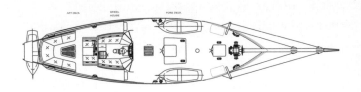

Top deck view of the *Mermaid*

The deck plan shows a wide expanse of foredeck for stowage and for passengers to roam around. The aft deck has a wraparound seat for lounging, and just aft of the pilot house is an outside steering station with all-around visibility.

Below aft is a generous galley and day head, with a large wraparound dinette right aft. The interior layout has a flexible-use space just forward of amidships. This can be used as a cargo hold, or as a workshop, or as extra berth space for passengers.

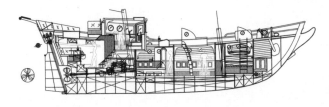

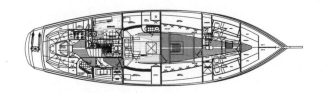

Side and top interior views of the *Mermaid*

The interior is arranged so that a couple can live aboard in relative privacy. With crew berths forward and crew access to the galley from the deck, there is no need for the owners to be disturbed.

An alternate arrangement would be to locate the owner's cabin right forward. This would move the cargo hold slightly farther aft. The crew quarters would then be just aft of amidships, and slightly less long. That would give the crew access to the engine room without disturbing the owners. It would also give the owners a completely private suite forward, out of the way of traffic and mayhem.

The center "cargo hold" could also be made into another king-size-berth luxury cabin for a shared ownership with another couple.

Power Boat Examples

The following examples illustrate the principles discussed in the "Power Boats" section on page 50.

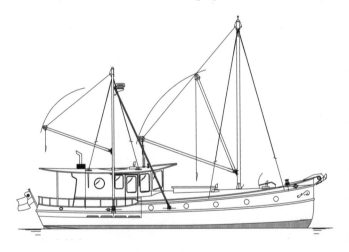

Side view of the *Roberta Jean*

This is the 43-foot motor yacht *Roberta Jean*. She has a robust steel structure and the profile is low, keeping the occupants closer to the roll axis. The pilot house is no more than ⅓ of the deck length, not counting the roof overhang aft, so presents the smallest possible windage area for the enclosed accommodations. Also, the pilot house is located just aft of amidships, the most comfortable spot in terms of pitch motions.

Paravane poles have been provided on the aft (mizzen) mast to lessen the boat's roll at sea. The foremast is arranged to take a steadying sail, and also has a cargo boom for lifting items aboard, such as a shore boat. The mizzen mast also has a boom for the same purpose.

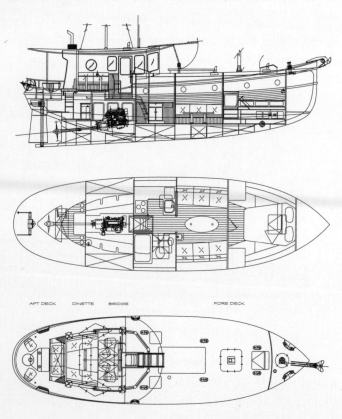

Side, top, and interior views of the *Roberta Jean*

The interior views show a good layout for two people, with additional berths for occasional guests on the settees, in the pilot house, and on the aft-facing seat on the aft deck.

Of course, it would be possible to squeeze in more accommodations, say by moving the settee seats inboard on one or both sides and providing a "pilot berth" above and outboard, but it is really much better to have an open, spacious interior.

Roberta Jean has a long flush foredeck. In other words, it extends all the way from one side to the other at the height of the bulwark top. This provides the maximum accommodation space below as well as enormous reserve buoyancy at large angles of heel. With this, the vessel is fully self-righting.

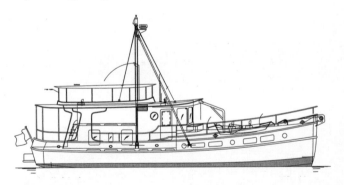

Side view of the *Vagrant*

The 49-foot *Vagrant* is a slightly larger steel motor yacht, intended for world voyaging. The pilot house is slightly longer than the *Roberta Jean*'s, amounting to about half the length on deck. The profile is still quite low, but this is about the maximum amount of windage that I would advocate for a true ocean-crossing power boat.

Again paravane poles are provided for roll attenuation. Above the pilot house is a removable canvas Bimini cover to provide shade to anyone occupying the uppermost "flying bridge" area. A second helm is provided on the flying bridge.

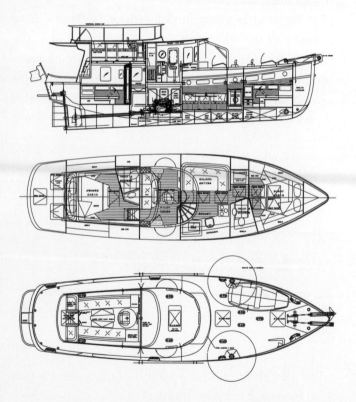

Side, interior, and deck views of the *Vagrant*

The objective here was to have a spacious open-air flying bridge for entertaining and to enjoy the view but also to limit the overall height in order to squeeze the vessel through the European canal system (the height restriction for old stone bridges is quite low). The Bimini cover can be removed when needed, and the mast, exhaust stack, and paravane rig lowered.

The interior drawings show a layout optimized for two couples or a couple with two children. In the case of having youngsters aboard, the forward cabin would have a pair of single berths, one on each side.

With two couples aboard, the spaces are well separated for privacy. There is plenty of common area: interior dinette, aft deck seats, and very spacious flying bridge. When the weather is fair it would be nice to sleep under the stars on the flying bridge.

A big plus with this kind of arrangement is that the engine room and bulk fuel tanks are located amidships. This keeps weight out of the ends, where excess weight can become a liability in terms of pitch behavior. It also keeps the fuel tanks central in order to limit trim issues as fuel is used over the course of a voyage.

Selected Resources for Supplies and Services

The following is my list of recommended suppliers, as well as a few websites that you may find helpful:

ICOM (www.icomamerica.com; communications equipment)

Icom America is a world leader in the amateur radio market, providing two-way radios for use in long-range (HF) and short-range (VHF, UHF) communications. They offer a wide range of portable, mobile, and base station/repeater radio options, as well as fully customizable systems. Icom's marine equipment includes long-range, ship-to-shore, single side-band (SSB) transceivers for worldwide communications, and the best in shorter-range VHF marine communications. The company has pioneered cutting-edge technology in the world of amateur radio, and their products feature state-of-the-art design elements.

FoodInsurance.com (www.foodinsurance.com; long-term food supplies)

FoodInsurance.com provides the finest prepackaged meals designed for long-term storage. Food Insurance products offer a guarantee against hunger, with great tasting, nutritious meals with 25-plus-year shelf lives, giving you the peace of mind that no matter what happens, you'll have quality sustenance.

MonsterFlashlight.com (www.monsterflashlight.com; LED flashlights)

MonsterFlashlight.com sells the finest tactical LED flashlights and associated gear serving even the most demanding needs.

Furuno USA (www.furunousa.com; marine electronics)

Since its inception in 1948, when the world's first fish finder was commercialized, Furuno Electric Co., Ltd., has been responding to the needs of the maritime industry through developing various types of marine electronics. Today, Furuno is a total marine electronics manufacturer operating on a global scale with a great many loyal customers.

Iridium (www.iridium.com; satellite communications)

Iridium Communications Inc. is the only satellite communications company that offers truly global voice and data communications coverage. Iridium's 66 low-earth-orbiting (LEO) cross-linked satellites make up the world's largest commercial constellation. Reaching over oceans, through airways, and across the polar regions, Iridium solutions are ideally suited for industries such as maritime, aviation, government/military, emergency/ humanitarian services, mining, forestry, oil and gas, heavy equipment, transportation, and utilities.

Kasten Marine Design, Inc. (www.kastenmarine.com; yacht design services)

Michael Kasten is a cutting-edge marine designer who offers a wide array of existing and custom design services. He has been creating quality metal, wood, and GRP boat designs, both power and sail, for over 25 years; nearly all of his boats are intended for long distance ocean voyaging, referred to as "nomadic watercraft." Kasten's recent designs include motorsailing craft for family voyaging and for carrying cargo or passengers. Mr. Kasten believes that everincreasing fuel prices make motorsailing the wave of the future.

Other Useful Websites:

www.SolarHam.com

www.fema.gov

www.williamesimpson.com

Index

Acknowledgments

The writing of *The Nautical Prepper* was as much about the patience of the people around me as it was my own, and I think we all learned why some authors need to retreat to the seclusion of a desert or mountaintop in order to complete a manuscript.

Nonetheless, had it not been for the generous and loving support and encouragement of my wife, Laura, and my family, William and Mequasah, Ciara and Jeremy, and Edwin, this book would still be just one of my many ideas.

Even though my parents are now deceased, I remain eternally grateful for a mother and father who taught me that life is like a roller coaster with many ups and downs, and if you persevere, you can do anything you set your mind to.

I am thankful for a country that still allows authors the freedom to write without worry of interference, prejudice, or censorship and for our past and present military personnel who selflessly and bravely serve to ensure that we all continue to have the rights that we are guaranteed under the constitution of the United States. And who I have no doubt will continue to do so in the future. I, for one, do not take those sacrifices and hard-earned rights for granted.

I would also like to express my sincere gratitude to the following people:

Mr. Alan Madison, executive producer for National Geographic's show *Doomsday Preppers*, for giving me the opportunity to appear on his show, which was the catalyst for the creation of this book.

Mr. Steve Hayes, of Quiet Productions, for his work and support on the project.

Mr. Robert Saberi, for his friendship and undying support and encouragement.

Mr. James Buchal, esq., for his sage advice and support.

Mr. Ray Riegert, Ms. Kelly Reed, Ms. Kourtney Joy, and everyone else at Ulysses Press for believing in me and signing me onboard as a new author with a first-class book deal.

Mr. Michael Kasten, a skilled naval architect for his contribution to this book (Chapter 2).

And I especially want to thank all my readers! Without your support it would be impossible for me to continue as an author.

Thank you!

About the Author

Capt. William E. Simpson II is a U.S. Merchant Marine Officer with decades of boating and expedition sailing experience, having logged more than 150,000 miles at sea. Capt. Simpson has successfully survived long-term "off the grid" at sea and on remote uninhabited desert islands with his family for years at a time. In early 2013, Capt. Simpson appeared on National Geographic's hit TV show *Doomsday Preppers* (Season 2, "A Fortress at Sea) and received the highest score ever given for disaster preparedness and survival, earning the title of "Best Prepper." He holds a U.S.C.G. 500-ton captain's license for commercial-inspected passenger vessels and is also a commercial airplane and helicopter pilot. In 1987 Capt. Simpson received a commendation from the U.S. Coast Guard Honolulu Sector for his assistance in the successful rescue of two sailors lost overboard at sea. In 2010, Capt. Simpson was again instrumental in the successful rescue operation of an American sailor lost overboard in the Sea of Cortez in hazardous waters. Capt. Simpson is also an accomplished writer covering disaster preparedness. His work has been featured and republished in numerous magazines and website,s and he has been a featured guest on various disaster preparedness radio talk shows.